ISAIAH

THE REDEMPTION OF THE LORD

But now thus saith Jehovah, that created thee, O Jacob, and he that formed thee, O Israel: Fear not, for I have redeemed thee, I have called thee by thy name; thou art mine.

—Isaiah 43:1

ISAIAH

THE REDEMPTION OF THE LORD

Stephen Kaung

Christian Fellowship Publishers, Inc.
New York

Paperback ISBN: 978-1-68062-121-1
eBook ISBN: 978-1-68062-122-8

Available from the Publishers at:

11515 Allecingie Parkway
Richmond, Virginia 23235
www.c-f-p.com

Printed in the United States of America

Preface

The New Testament quotes Isaiah more than any other book and mentions his name twenty-one times. The Lord Jesus and the early disciples all knew this book well and shared the good news from it. But for many of us, its sixty-six chapters and various prophecies are overwhelming. We begin to feel lost as we read, not knowing who or what it is talking about.

The Ethiopian eunuch was also confused as he pondered over Isaiah 53 (see Acts 8:26-39). When Philip asked him if he understood what he was reading, he shared how he needed someone to guide him. Then from that passage, Philip was able to announce the good news of Jesus to him.

Similarly, the nine chapters in this volume serve as a type of guide for discovering Christ in this largest prophetic book of the Bible. They unlock many confusing passages while also revealing our Savior. Beginning with Isaiah's life-changing vision of God, Stephen Kaung then considers some of the more famous passages about the birth of the Lord Jesus, His life, and His suffering at the cross. We are guided through Scriptures on the future kingdom as well as essential help for our present situation in the church.

As the Ethiopian found Christ through Isaiah and "went on his way rejoicing," may we too find Christ our Redeemer in Isaiah and be filled with joy at the discovery.

Contents

Preface 7
1—Isaiah's Vision of the Lord 11
2—Unto Us a Son is Given 27
3—His Scent Shall Be In the Fear of the LORD 43
4—In Returning and Rest 63
5—Comfort Ye, Comfort Ye My People 77
6—Behold My Servant 93
7—Who Hath Believed Our Report? 111
8—Keep Not Silence, Give Him No Rest 127
9—To the Afflicted and Contrite in Spirit 143

A series of messages on Isaiah was delivered by the author during the period of December 1974 to April 1975, before a group of Christians who gathered together for worship in Richmond, VA. Those recorded messages were transcribed for this publication.

Unless otherwise indicated,
Scripture quotations are from the
New Translation by J. N. Darby.

1—Isaiah's Vision of the Lord

Isaiah 6:1-13—In the year of the death of king Uzziah, I saw the Lord sitting upon a throne, high and lifted up; and his train filled the temple. Seraphim were standing above him: each had six wings; with twain he covered his face, and with twain he covered his feet, and with twain he flew. And one called to the other and said, Holy, holy, holy is Jehovah of hosts; the whole earth is full of his glory! And the foundations of the thresholds shook at the voice of him that cried, and the house was filled with smoke. And I said, Woe unto me! for I am undone; for I am a man of unclean lips, and I dwell in the midst of a people of unclean lips: for mine eyes have seen the King, Jehovah of hosts. And one of the seraphim flew unto me, and he had in his hand a glowing coal, which he had taken with the tongs from off the altar; and he made it touch my mouth, and said, Behold, this hath touched thy lips; and thine iniquity is taken away, and thy sin expiated.

And I heard the voice of the Lord saying, Whom shall I send, and who will go for us? And I said, Here am I; send me. And he said, Go; and thou shalt say unto this people, Hearing ye shall hear and shall not understand, and seeing ye shall see and shall not perceive. Make the heart of this people fat, and make their ears heavy, and blind their eyes; lest they see with their eyes, and hear with their ears, and understand with their heart, and be converted, and healed. And I said, Lord, how long? And he said, Until

> the cities be wasted, without inhabitant, and the houses without man, and the land become an utter desolation, and Jehovah have removed men far away, and the solitude be great in the midst of the land. But a tenth part shall still be therein, and it shall return and be eaten; as the terebinth and as the oak whose trunk remaineth after the felling: the holy seed shall be the trunk thereof.

The very name of the prophet Isaiah is meaningful. In Isaiah 8, he mentioned that he and his children are given as signs to the people (see v.18). Isaiah means, *Jehovah is salvation* or *the salvation of the LORD*.

No book of the Old Testament is quoted more in the New Testament than the book of Isaiah. This time we would like to consider together before the Lord the vision of Isaiah in chapter 6.

In the year of the death of king Uzziah

Some Bible scholars think that Isaiah and Uzziah were probably brothers or cousins because of the affinity of their names. If that was the case, Isaiah must have been very close to King Uzziah. If Isaiah was not his brother or his cousin, at least we know Isaiah was very close to Uzziah. Why? Because he wrote all the deeds of King Uzziah in his book. He was his friend, his chronicler. They were very close.

But when King Uzziah died, it evidently constituted a kind of crisis in the life of Isaiah. Whether Isaiah prophesied before chapter 6, we are not sure. There are prophecies in chapters 1 to 5, but we do not know whether these five chapters were words that he prophesied *before* he saw the Lord in chapter 6. If he did, then he had prophesied even before the year of the death of King Uzziah, but when King Uzziah died, it became a crisis to him as a prophet. If instead, he had never prophesied before chapter 6, then this year of the death of King Uzziah formed such a crisis in his life that from then on, he was called to be a prophet. Either way, the death of King Uzziah became a crisis to Isaiah.

Life is made up of crises. From time to time, a crisis will come to you. Generally speaking, life is such that you just cannot go on without any crisis. Maybe your friend or close relative died, or perhaps something else happened to you in your life. Life is full of crises.

There are spiritual crises too. These are very important times because if we can meet the crisis in the right way, we will come out on higher ground, but if we meet the crisis in the wrong way, then probably we will turn somewhere else. Crises are very important to us.

When a crisis comes into your life, whatever kind it may be, how are you going to face it? A crisis had come to the life of Isaiah, and it must have been a critical one. How did he meet that crisis? He did one thing—the only thing that is right—he entered into the temple to inquire of the Lord.

If a crisis comes to your life and you begin to look at it directly, and you look at yourself, or you even look around at other people, you won't be able to solve it the right way. This is the only way to face a crisis of any kind: enter into the temple and inquire of the Lord. Do not think that you can solve the problem. Do not even try to solve it. Go to the Lord and seek His face, then everything will be clear.

The Bible says that King Uzziah was not a bad king. He was a good king. He did everything right in the eyes of the Lord. And because of that, God prospered him (see II

Chronicles 26:4-5). Once he was prosperous, he became proud and did this one thing: he went into the temple to offer incense! (see v.16) From all outward appearances, this was not something bad. He was not sinning in any worldly sense. God had so blessed him that he wanted to go to the temple to offer incense to Him. He wanted to pray. He wanted to worship God! Now, this, to our reasoning, would be a good thing. But offering incense was the job of the priest, not of the king. Since he was so blessed, he became spiritually proud. He thought he could do everything. He entered into the temple to burn incense. And because of that, he was smitten with leprosy. That was his downfall. He had to live in a separate house, never again to enter into the temple, until he died.

Isaiah must have known very well what had happened to King Uzziah. The downfall of King Uzziah was entering into the temple to offer incense. You would think that Isaiah would have been afraid to go into the temple. But on the contrary, after the death of King Uzziah, Isaiah entered into the temple to face the crisis of his life.

Not being a priest, and knowing what had happened to King Uzziah, he certainly wouldn't have dared to burn incense; he wouldn't have dared to enter into the holy place. Though he may have been of royal seed, when he entered into the temple, he was just like any other of the children of Israel. He would be in the outer court.

In a sense, he was far away from the inner Holy of Holies, the holiest of all. There in the court, he prayed. He opened his heart to God. He cried unto the Lord. He was almost like that publican our Lord Jesus talked about in Luke 18. The Pharisee went to the temple and boasted of himself, but the publican stood afar off, beating his breast, saying, "O God, have compassion on me, the sinner" (v. 13).

Isaiah was probably standing at the back of the court. There he opened his heart to God. He cried unto God concerning the crisis. While he was praying, something happened. The veil opened. In the spirit, he was brought into the holiest of all!—the place where no one could enter, not even the priest. Once a year, the high priest could enter behind the veil for a short while with blood and the smoke of incense. He had to hurry out because no one could stand in the presence of God. As Isaiah prayed, the physical temple faded away, and he was taken by the Spirit into the holiest of all. There he saw the Lord sitting on the throne high and lifted up.

I saw the Lord sitting upon a throne,
high and lifted up

Behind the veil, in the holiest of all, there was the ark. Upon the ark was the mercy seat with two cherubim as the cover of the seat, and the glory of God sat on the mercy seat. No one was allowed to see this, yet Isaiah saw what people could not see. He saw the Lord sitting on the throne, high and lifted up.

Dear brothers and sisters, the physical is just a type; the spiritual is the reality. The earthly is just a shadow; the heavenly is the real thing. Here the earth, the physical, faded away. The spiritual and the heavenly appeared to Isaiah. He saw reality. And what is reality? Reality is: the Lord is on the throne, high and lifted up.

King Uzziah had died. The nation now entered into a period of change. Isaiah was probably wondering whether the change would be for better or for worse. Because of the death of King Uzziah, a change might come to Isaiah himself. He didn't know what kind of effect it would have upon him. He wondered about himself. He wondered about the nation. Everything would now be changing.

We are always afraid when things are changing because we are no longer sure. What can *really* stabilize us? When everything around us is changing, and we ourselves are changing, what can stabilize us? Only one vision—the Lord on the throne. Everything changes, but He remains the same—yesterday, today, and forever (Hebrews 13:8). Everything will be shaken, but there is a throne that never shakes (12:27). God is on that throne. He rules, and He overrules everything.

Brothers and sisters, we are living in a very critical day. We find changes all around us, and we are amazed at the swiftness of these changes. Things change very quickly today. And as we are surrounded by changes, as we ourselves are changing, where is our security? Where is our strength? Where is our stability? It is not in us. It is not around us. It is only in the Lord who sits on the throne. We know one thing: the Lord sits on the throne. We know one thing: He rules and overrules over all things. He is "high and lifted up." This much we know.

I believe we need to catch this vision today because only that will stabilize us, will give us strength, will give us faith to go on.

and his train filled the temple

In a royal court, the king would have a beautiful royal robe upon him. Then the very long train of that robe would spread out. Isaiah saw this in the vision. The Lord was sitting on the throne as the King of kings, and the train of His robe filled the temple.

The glory of the Lord was in the holiest of all, but it was hidden by a heavy veil that separated the holiest of all from the holy place. Nobody could see the glory of the Lord in the holy place. All they could see was the golden altar of incense, the golden table of shewbread, and the candlestick all of gold. Then in the court, they could see the brazen laver and the brazen altar at the entrance. They could see these things but not the glory of the Lord. It was hidden behind the veil. But in this vision, His "train filled the temple." The glory of the Lord came out, and His train filled the temple.

Now, what are these things that you see in the temple? The altar of incense, shewbread table, candlestick of gold, brazen laver, brazen altar—what are these things? These speak to us of the works of God in Christ Jesus. All these things in the temple speak of the works of our Lord Jesus, what the Lord has done.

He is the Brazen Altar. He shed His blood for the remission of our sins (see Matthew 26:28, Hebrews 9:22).

He is the Brazen Laver. He is our sanctification. He sanctifies us by "the washing of the water with the word" that He may present us to himself "a glorious church without spot or wrinkle or any such thing" (see Ephesians 5:26-27).

He is the Candlestick of Gold. He is our light. If we walk in the light as He is in the light, we have fellowship with one another (see I John 1:7). He is the light of life (see John 1:4).

He is <u>the Shewbread on the Table</u>. He is the bread of life. And if we eat of Him, we shall never die (see John 6:32-58).

He is <u>the Golden Table of Incense</u>. He is our Great High Priest (see Hebrews 4:14), making intercession for us. And He is able to save to the uttermost those who come by Him to God (see 7:25).

So you find that all these things in the temple speak of the works of our Lord Jesus. The train fills the temple. In other words, the works of the Lord Jesus fill the house.

What is God's temple, God's house today? It is the church. The Lord is on the throne, and His train fills the temple. The Lord is on the throne, and His work fills the church. He is working. He is working towards His purpose until His glory shall fill all the earth (see Isaiah 6:3 "the whole earth is full of his glory").

When everything is shaken, when change is coming, we wonder if God will ever get what He wants. We wonder if God is able to have His purpose realized. We look at ourselves, and we do not like what we see. It doesn't look like we can be that vessel for the purpose of God. But the Lord said, "I will build My church upon this rock, and the gates of Hades shall not prevail against it" (see Matthew 16:18b).

He is working. His work is to fill the church until He has obtained what He wants. It all begins from the throne. He is on the throne, and He is working from the throne out until His glory not only shall fill the temple, but His glory shall fill the whole earth.

Brothers and sisters, this is the vision that Isaiah saw. God is still on the throne. He is still working out His purpose.

He will work first through the church, and then His glory shall fill the earth.

Seraphim were standing above him

Isaiah saw the seraphim. This section of Scripture is the only place where seraphim are mentioned in the Bible. We do not know if seraphim are cherubim, or whether they are two different groups. The word seraphim means *burning ones.* They are the burning ones. In a sense, they stand for the holiness of God in relation to His people because they cry, "Holy, holy, holy, is Jehovah of Hosts, the whole earth is full of His glory!" (v.3)

Now let us look at these seraphim. They are very close to the throne of God, and yet they use two of their wings to cover their face. Though they are *burning ones*, they dare not look at God. They cover their faces as if they are ashamed of themselves. They use their other two wings to cover their feet. They dare not show their feet. They were faceless and feetless in the presence of God. With their other wings, they fly. As holy as these seraphim are—they are the *burning ones*—they dare not show their face before God. They cover their faces.

How about us? Dare we show our face before God? Should we not just cover our heads before God? We are nothing. We don't want people to look at us. We are covered, as if faceless before God. We dare not show our feet; we dare not walk in our own ways. If we walk in our own ways, we have gone astray. And like the two wings that fly, we are swift to worship God and to do His will.

And one called to the other and said,
Holy, holy, holy is Jehovah of hosts;
the whole earth is full of his glory!

These are the seraphim. And because they are so close to God, they cry out incessantly, one to another, "Holy, holy, holy is Jehovah of hosts." What is the meaning of holy? Just as being righteous is the opposite of sinning, holiness is the opposite of being common. Our God is holy, that is to say, He is uncommon—He is not like us; He is different, altogether different; He is unique; He is alone by himself; He is special; He is incomparable; He stands all by himself—*that* is holy.

Brothers and sisters, if we see God, if we see the Lord, one thing should be impressed upon us: He is different from us. Oftentimes, we make God like one of us, thinking that what we cannot do He cannot do and what we do not like He shouldn't like. Oh, but if we see the Lord, then we will know one thing: He is different. His ways are higher than our ways; His thoughts are higher than ours. He is just beyond us in all things. He is not common. He is unique.

He also knows what He is doing. Everything is in His hands. This is the same vision that Job saw at the end. After God spoke to Job, Job said, "Formerly I had only heard of Thee, but now I have seen Thee" (see Job 42:5). What did Job see? Job didn't see any explanation because God didn't explain his crisis. What did Job see? Job saw the holiness of God. God is holy. You don't argue with Him. His way is higher than your way, and His thought is higher than your thought (see Isaiah 55:9). All you do is bow down and repent. That's what you do.

This is also the same vision that the three disciples on the Mount of Transfiguration saw. They saw the Lord. Moses disappeared, Elijah disappeared, and the voice said, This is My Beloved Son, in whom I am well pleased, hear Him (see Matthew 17:1-8). He is unique! You cannot compare Him with Moses; you cannot compare Him with Elijah. He is different! Altogether different. He is all alone by himself. And all you can do is hear Him—don't talk—*hear* Him. That's the vision.

Oh, brothers and sisters, we need that vision! We need to see the Lord on the throne. We need to see His work fill the temple. We need to see that He is holy, unique. We have to cry out, "Holy, holy, holy, You are so different. You are so unique. You are so special. Jehovah of hosts."

holy is Jehovah of hosts

He is the Lord of hosts. He not only has heavenly hosts, but He also has earthly hosts. His heavenly hosts are the angels that will listen and carry out His will. His earthly host today is the church. It is for us to hear, to obey, to believe, and to do the will of God. And the result is,

the whole earth is full of his glory!

Oh, brothers and sisters, we are living at a time of much discouraging news and discouraging things. But thank God, there is one thing that will give us strength, spiritual strength, to stand against all changes—the vision of God. It is the vision of the Lord that gives us hope. Thank God, He is on the throne. He is working out His purpose. And He is working out His purpose through His church. We may fail, but He will never fail. One day His glory shall fill the earth as water fills the sea (see Habakkuk 2:14). He is doing this.

And I said, Woe unto me! for I am undone

When Isaiah saw this vision, what was the effect of it? After the cry of these seraphim—holy, holy, holy—the foundations of the threshold of the temple shook. The temple was filled with smoke, and Isaiah shook too! Isaiah was completely shaken. He was shattered. He said,

> Woe to me! for I am undone. I am a man of unclean lips, and I live among a people with unclean lips.

No one can see the Lord and remain standing. Even when Daniel, the beloved of the Lord, saw the Lord, he said, "My beauty has turned into corruption" (see Daniel 10:8). When you see the Lord, your beauty will turn into corruption.

What was the strongest point in the life of Isaiah? His lips. He must have talked a lot. That was his strongest point, and that was the very point at which he was shaken and shattered before God. "Woe to me, I am altogether woeful. Nothing good is in me! Especially one thing: my lips. My lips are unclean, unclean!"

If he was a prophet before that vision, then, of course, a prophet has to use his lips. And if you look into the first five chapters of the book of Isaiah, you find how strongly he prophesied. That was his strength! Even though in his prophesying, there was nothing wrong, yet when he saw the Lord, he said, "My lips were wrong, unclean. When God's word came from my lips, it carried my uncleanness. It was impure."

And he said, "I live among a people of unclean lips." People are always talking, and they might be talking about the Lord, but it is unclean, unclean. Brothers and sisters, if we see the Lord, then we find that in the holiest things that we do, there are unclean lips. One brother once said, "Even our repentance needs to be washed with the blood." It's not pure.

Who can see the Lord and not be undone? If someone says he has seen the Lord and he can still stand up, then you know he hasn't seen the Lord. If he had seen the Lord, he would be as one dead, prostrating himself upon the floor, repenting in dust and ashes. You cannot help it.

Behold, this hath touched thy lips

> And one of the seraphim flew unto me, and he had in his hand a glowing coal, which he had taken with the tongs from off the altar; and he made it touch my mouth, and said, Behold, this hath touched thy lips; and thine iniquity is taken away, and thy sin expiated (vv. 6-7)

Because of this repentance, one of the seraphim came, used a tong, took a piece of glowing coal, a lump of live coal, off of the altar, touched his lips, and said, "Your lips are clean, your sins are expiated." God had not shown himself to Isaiah to destroy him. God revealed himself to Isaiah to complete him. After Isaiah repented in dust and ashes, God cleansed him.

And I heard the voice of the Lord saying,
Whom shall I send, and who will go for us?

Then Isaiah heard the voice, "Whom shall I send? Who will go for us?" This is the calling. Brothers and sisters, we need to see the Lord. And if we see the Lord, we will hear the calling. The calling was not, "Isaiah, Isaiah, I want you." No. The calling was just as if God was speaking to himself. It was as if there was a conversation in the Godhead. Among the Godhead, they were asking, "Now whom shall we send? Who will go for us? There is something that needs to be done; some message needs to be delivered to the children of Israel. But whom can we send? Who will go for us?" They were talking among the Godhead. And it was as if Isaiah overheard them talking. That's the way it is. God did not speak to Isaiah directly. God was speaking among the Godhead, and Isaiah overheard it.

And I said, Here am I; send me.

So Isaiah said, "Well, here am I. Send me." We often say that God never wants volunteers. He always drafts people. We often do volunteer for God. God said, "I don't want volunteers. If I need someone, I will draft him." You don't volunteer. God drafts!

But this is only half of the truth. The whole truth is, God drafts, and we volunteer! So here, God is drafting, and Isaiah volunteered. That's the way it happens.

Do you overhear God's burden? If you overhear God's burden, then you cannot but volunteer though you may know you are unfit. People may think they volunteer because they are qualified. No. You volunteer because you are not qualified. You know you are not qualified, and yet you volunteer. Why? Because you have heard God's burden. You cannot escape.

And he said, Go

So Isaiah volunteered and said, "Here am I, send me." And you know the mission that God sent Isaiah to fulfill was an impossible mission. God said, "All right, you go and tell My people: They have ears, and yet they cannot hear. They have eyes, and yet they cannot see. They will not understand. There will be judgment upon them. Though there remains a remnant, they will still be judged" (see vv. 9-13).

There was no hope. Now, who wants to bring that kind of message? That will be very uncomfortable. Who would be willing to bring such a message and make himself so unpopular? Only a person who is broken before God, taken into the secret counsel of God, and is one in heart with God.

You may want to change the message a little bit to make it a little milder. But no, that would be unclean. To be a prophet, you have to prophesy just as God tells you: "There is no hope for the children of Israel. It is absolutely hopeless." But where is the hope? The hope is in God, in the Messiah. That's why in the book of Isaiah, there is no hope so far as the children of Israel were concerned. But thank God, He said their hope was in Christ.

This is the same with us today. Oh, brothers and sisters, if we know the burden of the Lord, we too have to say that so far as we are concerned, it is a hopeless situation. There is no hope. But thank God, there is hope! The hope is in Christ. Only in Christ will you find salvation, restoration, and fulfillment. May the Lord also give us a vision of God, and with it, a mission to fulfill.

2—Unto Us a Son is Given

> Isaiah 9:6-7—For unto us a child is born, unto us a son is given; and the government shall be upon his shoulder; and his name is called Wonderful, Counsellor, Mighty God, Father of Eternity, Prince of Peace. Of the increase of his government and of peace there shall be no end, upon the throne of David and over his kingdom, to establish it, and to uphold it with judgment and with righteousness, from henceforth even for ever. The zeal of Jehovah of hosts will perform this.

The prophet Isaiah lived around 800 BC approximately. He was almost midway between the time of Moses and Christ. Of all the Old Testament prophets, none was given such a full revelation concerning Christ. We can say that Isaiah is the Paul of the Old Testament.

Throughout his book, there are many prophecies concerning Christ, especially in the second part of Isaiah (chapters 40-66). But even in the first part of Isaiah, we find these great prophecies concerning Christ, which we may all be familiar with:

> Therefore will the Lord himself give you a sign: Behold, the virgin shall conceive and shall bring forth a son, and call his name Immanuel (7:14).

This is a tremendous prophecy concerning Christ!

> For unto us a child is born, unto us a son is given; and the government shall be upon his shoulder ... (9:6a).
>
> And there shall come forth a shoot out of the stock of Jesse, and a branch out of his roots shall be fruitful; and the Spirit of Jehovah shall rest upon him (11:1-2a).
>
> In that day will Jehovah of hosts be for a crown of glory, and for a diadem of beauty, unto the remnant of his people; and for a spirit of judgment to him that sitteth in judgment, and for strength to them that turn the battle to the gate (28:5-6).

So Isaiah prophesied a great deal about Christ. And for this chapter, we would like to concentrate on the two verses we read in the beginning.

unto us a child is born, unto us a son is given

During this month (December), people's minds are occupied with Christmas. They are preparing for Christmas Day. I suppose we all know that the Bible is silent on the exact day of the birth of Christ. People celebrate Christmas on December 25th, not because the Bible says to, but from a tradition that originated with the heathen world.

The winter solstice happens on the 21st or 22nd of December. This is the shortest day of the year, the longest night. The heathens used to have a kind of superstition about it. They were afraid that the Sun would go down and never come up again. That would mean death. When the Sun began to rise (after December 22nd) and even to stay longer, they were so happy about it that they took December 25th as the birthday of the sun-god Mithra.

Later on, Christianity just Christianized or baptized that heathen day and made it the birthday of Christ, assuming that Christ is the "Sun of Righteousness" (see Malachi 4:2). This is the origin of December 25th as the birthday of Christ.

The Bible does exhort us to remember the death of the Lord but never asks us to celebrate His birth. But we are not trying to argue over this matter of the date of His birth. I think that is a minor issue. What is important is the fact of the birth of our Lord Jesus. With that fact is tremendous meaning.

The prophet Isaiah prophesied about 800 years before the birth of Christ: "For unto us a child is born, unto us a son is given ..." A child, a son, is born, is given.

"A child is born"—speaks of the humanity of our Lord Jesus. He was born into this world as a child. He was born as a baby. He had to grow up from babyhood to adolescence until he became a full-grown man. He had to go through all the stages of human life. He is a man, a perfect man. And because of that, He is able to sympathize with us (see Hebrews 4:15). He can die for us on the cross. "... unto us a child is born ..."

"... unto us a son is given"– speaks of His divinity. The Child who is to be born is the Son that is given. In other words, before the Child is born, He was the Son. He is the eternal Son of God:

> For God so loved the world, that He gave *His only begotten Son*, that whosoever believeth in Him should not perish, but have everlasting life (John 3:16 KJV emphasis added).

This phrase "a son is given" speaks of the divinity of our Lord Jesus. He is God. He is "… perfect God." And because of the love of God, He is given to the world that we might be saved.

Now, brothers and sisters, this is a tremendous fact. It is now a historical fact. When Isaiah said these words, it was a prophecy, but as we read this word, it is an accomplished fact—history. "Unto us a child is born, unto us a son is given." There is tremendous love behind this fact.

But I would like to ask one question: Why is the child born? Why is the son given? The child is born *unto us*; the son is given *unto us*. That is to say, it is not just that He is born and that's it, or He is given, and that's it. He is born *unto us*. He is given *unto us*. So the question is: Is He born so far as we are concerned? Is He given? Have we received Him? If we have received Him, then He is born in us, and we are born again. This is the salvation that He brings into this world.

and the government shall be upon his shoulder

Oftentimes, we think of how Christ was born, how the Son was given so that we may be saved. And thank God for that! That is true. The personal aspect of the birth of Christ, of the giving of the Son, is our salvation. It is so that we may be saved. But there is another overall aspect that we often overlook that is contained here in the prophecy of Isaiah.

"For unto us a child is born, … a son is given"—for what reason? For what purpose? "… and the government shall be upon his shoulder." In other words, this Child that is born, this Son that is given, is to have the government upon His shoulder. He is not only born and given to be our Savior—and thank God He is!—but He is born to be King. He is born to have government upon His shoulder. He is born to establish His kingdom upon this earth. That is the overall aspect of the birth of Christ.

This is the Gospel according to Matthew. When you open the New Testament, you find the Gospel according to Matthew, the first Gospel. And the first Gospel is: He is born to be King. Even when He was judged, He said, "I am born a king" (see John 18:37). But His kingdom is not of this world (see v. 36). He came to establish His kingdom upon this earth; that is what He was born for.

"... and the government"—What government? The government of God, the government of the kingdom of God—"shall be upon His shoulder." Now let's go back a little bit concerning the government of God. God is the creator of the heavens and the earth. And after He had finished creating the heavens and the earth, He created man. He created man in His own image. And then He gave dominion over the fowl of the air, the cattle of the field, and the fishes of the sea, into the hands of man (see Genesis 1). In other words, God gave the government of this earth to man that man might rule this earth for Him, might subdue the earth, might bring this earth back to the glory of God. That was how the government on earth was first handed to man by his Maker.

But unfortunately, man sinned. Man failed. And because of this, dominion passed out of the hands of man. Man not only lost God's image but also lost the dominion that God had first given to him. And because of this, Satan is now called the prince of this world (see John 12:31). In other words, he took from man the government that God first put into the hands of man.

But that does not mean that God just gave up His government. God began to react. And when God began to react, first, He called a man by the name of Abraham. Abraham, the "father of faith" (see Romans 4:11-12). From that man, He began to raise up a nation. And this nation of Israel was to be God's kingdom on the earth. When they were in the wilderness, after being delivered out of Egypt, the prophet Balaam prophesied about them:

> He hath not beheld iniquity in Jacob, neither hath he seen wrong in Israel; Jehovah his God is with him, and the shout of a king is in his midst (Numbers 23:21).

God had redeemed a people out of Egypt. God brought them to himself, and God was their King. The shout of the King was in their midst. God was their King. God had His government over a people on this earth, and these people were the children of Israel.

This was fully fulfilled in the time of David. When David was king, he was king as representative of God. God was actually the King over the nation of Israel. But unfortunately, the children of Israel were unfaithful to God. And because of that, the nation was taken into Babylonian captivity.

Government again came into the hand of the Gentiles, beginning with Babylon. During that period of the Old Testament, God was never called "the God of the heavens and the earth." He was always addressed only as "the God of the heavens." He was not called the God of the earth because no nation could represent His government.

In the book of Daniel, we read, "the heavens do rule" (see 4:26). Even though government was in the hand of the Gentiles, yet the heavens still ruled. But the heavens did not rule directly, the heavens ruled indirectly. The heavenly government was an invisible thing. It was not seen on this earth. This continued for about a thousand years until the time of Christ.

When Christ was born, when this Son of God was given, something began on earth which is of tremendous consequence. When Christ was born, God began a new move: to establish His kingdom upon this earth, and this government shall be upon His shoulders.

When you open the New Testament, you find the forerunner of Christ, John the Baptist. When he came out to preach, what was his message? "Repent, for the kingdom of the heavens is at hand" (see Matthew 3:2). Why should the children of Israel repent? Because the kingdom of the heavens was at hand. God was going to establish His kingdom upon this earth.

And when Christ first preached the gospel, He did the same thing. He said, "Repent for the kingdom of the heavens is at hand" (see Matthew 4:17). Why? Because the King was now in their midst. And if any should accept Him as their King, they would be His kingdom. Over them, He would rule because government is upon His shoulder.

The Jews at that time were looking for a physical kingdom. They expected a physical kingdom to be established without any spiritual preparation. But when God makes a move, He always brings in spiritual reality before the physical manifestation. Since they were looking for a physical kingdom, they were not prepared to repent. They did not have the spiritual preparation that was necessary for the physical manifestation. And that is the reason why they rejected Jesus as their Messiah. They rejected Christ.

Of the increase of his government ...
there shall be no end

Even with the rejection of His government by the Jews, Christ began to gather around himself a people. First, the twelve disciples. Then 120 gathered on the day of Pentecost. Gradually they began to increase, and increase, and increase—first, in Jerusalem, then spreading through all of Judea and Samaria, and finally unto the ends of this earth (see Acts 1:8). The increase of His government shall know no end, but it began with the birth of Christ. It began with the coming of the Son.

One thing that we always need to remember is that the coming of Christ was for the establishment of God's kingdom upon this earth. That was the purpose of His birth. He was to establish a kingdom, though not of this world, yet upon this earth. He was to gather around himself a people. Over those people, He would have absolute rule. These are to be a people that will put themselves under His government. This is the purpose of His birth.

Brothers and sisters, we have believed in the Lord Jesus, we have accepted Him as our personal Savior. Thank God for that. But remember, this is just the beginning. We are saved that we may become His people, that we may become His kingdom, that He may exercise His government upon us, over us. Is this true with us today?

What is it that the Lord is doing today? He is bringing to himself a people who will give themselves entirely to Him that He may have complete control over them. His government shall be established among these people. This is the kingdom of God on the earth today. The church, in its spiritual reality, is the kingdom of God on earth today. Once He gains a people, He will gain His church. And when that body is fully matured, then He will return and bring His kingdom to be publicly manifested upon this earth. But first, there must be the spiritual realization of that kingdom upon this earth. This is why it is so important to us today. If we are waiting for the return of Christ to establish His kingdom publicly on earth, we must first allow Him to establish His kingdom among us and within us. There is a tremendous responsibility with every one of us. How we need to submit ourselves! How we need to yield our life completely to Christ and let His government be over us! If He should obtain that among us, then He will come and manifest His kingdom to this whole world.

his name is called ...

Since there is such a work to be done, Isaiah said, "and his name is called Wonderful, Counsellor, Mighty God, Father of Eternity, Prince of Peace." These are His titles. And these titles speak of His works. What is He going to do so that He may establish His kingdom upon this earth? What will He do so that He may have His government over mankind? His works are represented by these different titles.

Wonderful

His name being called *Wonderful* is connected to God's purpose. God's purpose is wonderful. In Romans 11, after Paul had shared the glorious gospel of Jesus Christ, he concluded with these words, "O depth of riches both of the wisdom and knowledge of God! how unsearchable his judgments, and untraceable his ways!" (v. 33) When you think of the riches, of the wisdom and knowledge of God, when you think of God's eternal purpose, it is beyond our understanding, it is wonderful!—really wonderful!

In the Old Testament time, in Judges 13, Samson's father Manoah asked the angel that appeared to him what his name was. The angel said, "Why do you ask my name? is it not Wonderful?" (see vv. 17-18). Our God is wonderful!

The word wonderful can also be translated as marvelous. He is just marvelous. He surprises us on all hands. We cannot comprehend the wonder of His purpose. Oh, His purpose is wonderful! Think of that. If you read the book of Ephesians, you find that the eternal purpose of God is really beyond our comprehension. Why? It is so wonderful. He will obtain for himself a people, a body, a bride, a habitation, in men! That He would join us to himself as one—now that is really wonderful! So when you think of Christ, you think of Him as wonderful. This is connected with purpose.

Counselor

The name Counselor is always connected with plan—you counsel and you lay down a plan.

> Plans are established by counsel; and with good advice make war (Proverbs 20:18).

He is the Counselor, and who can be His counselor? None (see Isaiah 40;13; Romans 11:34; I Corinthians 2:16). Here again, in Ephesians, God has an eternal purpose, and He has His counsel: "according to the counsel of His will" (1:11). He lays down a plan, a wonderful plan.

Mighty God

He is called Mighty God. Mighty God is always connected with work. After you have a purpose, you lay down a plan, and then you start to work. You start to work according to the counsel of His will, according to the eternal purpose of God. Mighty speaks of strength. He is not only great in wisdom as the Wonderful Counselor (see Isaiah 28:29 "he is wonderful in counsel, great in wisdom"), He is also great in might (see Jeremiah 10:6 "thy name is great in might," and also 32:19 "great in counsel and mighty in work"). He is the Mighty God.

Father of Eternity

In some versions, you may read "eternal father" or "everlasting father." In the original language, it is Father of Eternity. Why? Because this is a title. The Father and the Son are one, but the Father is the father, and the Son is the son. Sometimes people use this verse and say that because Christ is called "Eternal Father" or "Everlasting Father," therefore, the Son *is* the Father, and the Father *is* the Son. Remember this, the Father and the Son are one (see John 17:22), but the Father is the father, and the Son is the son.

He is called Father of Eternity. What does that mean? We say that George Washington is the father of the United States of America. He is the founder of this country. Thomas Edison was called "the father of the electricity age." The term father simply means that something begins with him. He represents it. He is the founder of it.

Our Lord Jesus is the father of eternity. Why? Because He *is* eternal life. And He gives eternal life to all those who believe in Him. Therefore He is called the Father of Eternity.

That is what He has done and is doing. So the name Father of Eternity is connected with grace. The grace of God in Christ Jesus is eternal life. We may have eternal life by believing in Him.

Prince of Peace

Finally, His name is called Prince of Peace. This speaks of the ultimate realization. He is our Peace. He makes peace for us with God and with one another (see Ephesians 2:14-15, Romans 5:1). And one day, His peace shall rule over this whole world. The world today does not have peace. How can they have peace if they reject the Prince of Peace? Our Lord Jesus is the only one who can bring peace into this world. Not just the cry of "peace, peace" (see Jeremiah 6:14), but real peace. And unless there is peace with God and with one another, there can be no peace in this world.

So here in these different names or titles, we are told of the works that He will do to bring His kingdom upon this earth.

Of the increase of his government
and of peace there shall be no end

The increase of His government shall know no end. It will increase and increase. It begins with very little. As we said before, He began with just twelve disciples. But then it continues to increase and to increase. More and more people will be constrained by His love to put themselves under His government. His government shall grow, and grow, and grow. The measure of the increase of His government shall be the measure of the increase of peace.

upon the throne of David
and over his kingdom

David is a type of the One who is greater than David (see Luke 20:44). David's kingdom is just a type of the kingdom that Christ will establish among men.

> ... to establish it, and to uphold it with judgment and with righteousness, from henceforth even for ever.

Daniel 2 shows us the historically prophetic vision of the kingdom of God. There Nebuchadnezzar saw an image with a gold head, silver breast, brass belly, iron legs, and partly iron and partly clay feet. Then in that vision, Nebuchadnezzar saw a stone that was not cut out with the hand of man. This stone will hit the feet of that great image, and the whole image will be shattered and disappear. The stone will then grow and increase and fill the earth. That prophetic vision is the history of the kingdom of God. The stone speaks of Christ and how Christ will destroy all the kingdoms of this earth. "The kingdoms of this earth shall become the kingdom of God and of His Christ" (see Revelation 11:15), and He shall fill this earth (see Habakkuk 2:14). That is the historical vision, and we know that this will happen very soon.

But here in Isaiah, it speaks of the spiritual reality of that kingdom. And the spiritual reality of that kingdom happens throughout the ages. You find that the increase of His government and of His peace shall know no end. In other words, it is increasing all the time.

Our Lord Jesus said, "I will build My church upon this rock. And the gates of Hades shall not prevail against it" (see Matthew 16:18). Sometimes we may not see much happening outwardly, but we do thank God that He is working towards His purpose. We do thank God that His government is increasing. And since His government is increasing, one day His kingdom shall publicly be manifested upon this earth—"from henceforth even forever." It never ends. It is going on all the time. If we have the eyes of faith, we shall see that His government is increasing. His kingdom is being established. He will establish His kingdom and uphold it with judgment and with righteousness.

to uphold it with judgment

What is judgment? How does He judge? He will judge and measure everything according to himself. He is the measuring rod. He is the rod of judgment. To bring us into His kingdom, to establish His government over us, He has to judge us. He has to measure us with himself. And when He measures us with himself, and we do not measure up, He has to discipline us. He has to deal with us. His dealings are to bring us to His measure that we may grow into the fullness of the measure of Christ.

and with righteousness

And what is that righteousness? The righteousness that is spoken here is what we find in Matthew.

> But seek ye first the kingdom of God and his righteousness, and all these things shall be added unto you (Matthew 6:33).

What is the kingdom of God and His righteousness?

> For I say unto you, that unless your righteousness surpass that of the scribes and Pharisees, ye shall in no wise enter into the kingdom of the heavens (Matthew 5:20).

And the Lord said, "You have heard that it has been said … but I say unto you …" (see Matthew 5-6). That is the righteousness of the kingdom, the "righteousnesses of the saints" (see Revelation 19:8).

Christ is building himself in us. He is reproducing himself in us. As we allow him to reproduce himself in us, His righteousness shall become our righteousness. This is the righteousness that is spoken of here. You can find it in Matthew 5-7. This is the righteousness of the kingdom: love your enemy, give to those who ask, pray for those who persecute you, etc. These are the righteousnesses of the kingdom.

from henceforth even for ever.

And He is to establish and to uphold His government, His kingdom, "with judgment and with righteousness, from henceforth even for ever."

So dear brothers and sisters, we do thank the Lord that about two thousand years ago, a child was born, a son was given. What tremendous result comes from that birth, from that giving! Throughout these two thousand years, we find the increase of His government. It continues on until He shall come back and manifest His kingdom and His government publicly on this earth.

The zeal of Jehovah of hosts will perform this.

The zeal of God, coupled with the power of God, will perform this. May we have faith in this. May we thank God that the zeal of God will perform this. This is coming, and this shall be fully realized.

In these days, as people's minds are occupied with Christmas, it behooves us to go back to the word of God. Let us seriously consider the meaning of the birth of that child, the giving of that son. May we yield ourselves more completely to Him that His government may truly be over us. Then as we are spiritually His kingdom we can pray, "Thy kingdom come, Thy will be done on earth as it is in heaven."

3—His Scent Shall Be In the Fear of the LORD

Isaiah 11:1-10—And there shall come forth a shoot out of the stock of Jesse, and a branch out of his roots shall be fruitful; and the Spirit of Jehovah shall rest upon him, the spirit of wisdom and understanding, the spirit of counsel and might, the spirit of knowledge and of the fear of Jehovah. And his delight will be in the fear of Jehovah; and he shall not judge after the sight of his eyes, neither reprove after the hearing of his ears; but with righteousness shall he judge the poor, and reprove with equity the meek of the earth: and he shall smite the earth with the rod of his mouth, and with the breath of his lips shall he slay the wicked. And righteousness shall be the girdle of his reins, and faithfulness the girdle of his loins. The wolf also shall dwell with the lamb, and the leopard shall lie down with the kid, and the calf and the young lion and the fatted beast together, and a little child shall lead them. And the cow and the she-bear shall feed; their young ones shall lie down together; and the lion shall eat straw like the ox. And the sucking child shall play on the hole of the adder, and the weaned child shall put forth its hand to the viper's den. They shall not hurt nor destroy in all my holy mountain; for the earth shall be full of the knowledge of Jehovah, as the waters cover the sea. And in that day there shall be a root of Jesse, standing as a banner of the peoples: the nations shall seek it; and his resting-place shall be glory.

In the original Hebrew text of the Bible, there were no divisions of chapters and verses. They came later on and are arbitrary. They are often helpful, but sometimes they seem to cover up the thought that God may want us to see. As we begin this chapter, the first word is "And"—"And there shall come forth a shoot out of the stock of Jesse." This word "and" shows us that it is a continuation of what has preceded this. To get the right impression of this passage, we have to see the continuity of thought there. In the preceding words, God disciplined His people Israel because of their unfaithfulness. And He used a very strange instrument to discipline His own people. He raised up the Assyrians as the rod of His anger.

> Ah! the Assyrian! the rod of mine anger! and the staff in their hand is mine indignation. I will send him against a hypocritical nation, and against the people of my wrath will I give him a charge; to take the spoil, and to seize the prey, and to tread them down like the mire of the streets (Isaiah 10:5-6).

God raised up and used the Assyrians as the rod of His anger to punish His own people. Why? Because His own people were a hypocritical nation. God disciplined His own with the enemy. But unfortunately, the Assyrians, the enemy, did not realize that it was God who used them to discipline His people. They thought that they were mighty and could do anything they liked to.

> But he meaneth not so, neither doth his heart think so; for it is in his heart to extirpate and cut off nations not a few (v.7).

While the Assyrians were being used by God, they thought that they were the mighty ones. And instead of executing the will of God, they desired to do things for themselves. Oftentimes they overdid it. That was the situation. So the Assyrians came, they conquered the nation of Israel, and yet they did more than they should have to God's people.

Now when such a situation was created, how would God react? God had reacted *against* His people, His unfaithful people, by raising up the Assyrians. But the Assyrians had overdone themselves. So now God reacted again *for* His people *against* His enemy. How did God react? What was God's reaction? We find it in the passage that we read in the eleventh chapter:

> And there shall come forth a shoot out of the stock of Jesse, and a branch out of his roots shall be fruitful (v.1).

When God reacts, He does not just react against a situation. He does not just react with another act. You find that when God reacts, He reacts with a person. In other words, His reaction is in a person. He reacts in every situation with a person, and that person is our Lord Jesus Christ.

The principle of divine reaction is not just an action; it is a Person. Whenever God really reacts, He always reacts with a Person. That Person is His total reaction to all situations. And that Person is our Lord Jesus Christ.

In your own experience, when God reacts in your life, in your situations, in the things you are involved with, do you think God just reacts with another action? And that's it? No. Whenever God really reacts, He always reacts with His Son. He always brings in His Son. His Son *is* the reaction to all actions, to all things. And in this case, with the nation of Israel, this principle is very evident.

And there shall come forth
a shoot out of the stock of Jesse

God reacted by raising up a shoot out of the stock of Jesse. We would like to ask this question: Why doesn't the Bible say, "There shall come forth a shoot out of the stock *of David*"? The Lord Jesus is the "son of David" (Matthew 21:9), and the son of David is greater than David because He also is the Lord of David (see Mark 12:35-37). Why should the prophet say a shoot out of the stock *of Jesse*, instead *of David*?

We know that David was a king who reigned and ruled. And yet when Israel was disciplined by God because of their unfaithfulness, the nation was destroyed. The royal seed was not only taken into captivity but even after they did return, the house of David was in its lowest state. Before Christ was born, where was the royal seed of David? What was the condition of David's seed? Joseph. David's seed was a carpenter living in Nazareth, not in Jerusalem. Instead of sitting on the throne of David, he was a carpenter. A carpenter! And he was hidden somewhere in the hills of obscure Nazareth—unknown.

The house of David was reduced to a very low standard. This is probably why we read "out of the stock of Jesse." God reacted at a time when the house of David was in its lowest state. He says, "out of the stock of Jesse" because Jesse was a commoner. It wasn't until David that this family became royal. So out of the stock of Jesse there came forth a shoot.

and a branch out of his roots shall be fruitful

This speaks of the humanity of our Lord Jesus. God reacted by bringing in His own Son. When His Son was brought into this world, He was born of the family of Jesse. He came as a man, as a human being just like we are. How He, the Son of God, emptied himself, and took upon himself the form of a man! (see Philippians 2:7) He was a man just like we are, and yet He was very fruitful—"his roots shall be fruitful."

and the Spirit of Jehovah shall rest upon him

What characterized this Man? Why was this Man different from any other man? "And the Spirit of Jehovah shall rest upon him." I believe this was fulfilled at the time when Jesus was baptized. When Jesus came to John the Baptist to be baptized, at first, John the Baptist refused to baptize Him. Somehow John the Baptist sensed the dignity that was in Jesus. He felt that this man was greater than he. He should be baptized by Him, instead of baptizing Him. So he refused to baptize Jesus. And then the Lord Jesus said, Do it, for the sake of righteousness. And John did it (see Matthew 3:13-15). After Jesus was baptized and came out of the water, heaven was opened, and the Holy Spirit descended and rested upon Him as a dove.

In the Old Testament time, the Spirit of God sometimes came upon a particular person and gave him a special gift or ability to do certain things. But never did the Holy Spirit, the Spirit of God, come into any man and dwell permanently with that person. Never. Some prophets, some kings, some great leaders—to them, the Holy Spirit would come and enable them to do great things. Yet the Holy Spirit never took up His abode in any of them.

Now you do find a few special cases. Let me just mention one man, David. One day David prayed a prayer of repentance. In Psalm 51, he asked the Lord, "Do not take the Holy Spirit away from me" (see v. 11). With David it does seem as if the Holy Spirit was given to him, yet, even so, it wasn't permanent. The Holy Spirit could come, and He could go. But not so with our Lord Jesus. The Lord Jesus was the first man upon whom the Spirit of God descended and took up His abode. The Holy Spirit rested in Him permanently.

When John saw this, he bore witness and testified that "this is the Son of God." How did John the Baptist know that Jesus is the Son of God? Because he was told, "Upon whom the Spirit shall descend and abide, this is the One who shall baptize with the Holy Spirit." So when he saw it, he bore witness and said, "This is the Son of God" (see John 1:32-34).

Our Lord Jesus, as a man, was filled with the Holy Spirit. He and the Holy Spirit are one. And God gave Him the Holy Spirit "without measure"(see John 3:34). And this Spirit that was in Him was described as the seven-fold Spirit:

> the Spirit of Jehovah shall rest upon him, the spirit of wisdom and understanding, the spirit of counsel and might, the spirit of knowledge and of the fear of Jehovah.

It is not that there are seven Holy Spirits. The Holy Spirit is one Spirit. But the Holy Spirit is so full and complete that there is the seven-foldness of the Holy Spirit.

This is just like what you see in the book of Revelation. Before the throne, there were seven torches burning, which are the seven spirits of God (see 4:5). These actually are one Spirit, but seven-fold. Seven in the Scripture always speaks of fulness, completeness.

the spirit of Jehovah

The "spirit of Jehovah" means the Spirit of the God who covenanted with man. And some commentators think that "the spirit of Jehovah" especially emphasizes the spirit of prophecy.

the spirit of wisdom and understanding

The Holy Spirit of inspiration is the spirit of wisdom and understanding. Now, wisdom and understanding form a pair. It is very difficult to distinguish between wisdom and understanding. One man put it this way, "Wisdom is the power of discerning the nature of things through their appearances." We see things by their appearance. But if all we see are the appearances on the surface, then it is superficial knowledge. There is not much wisdom in it. Wisdom penetrates behind the appearance of things and reveals to us the true nature of that thing. That is wisdom.

What is understanding? The same man said, "Understanding is the power of discerning the differences between things in their appearances." Wisdom is discerning *the true nature* of a thing. Understanding is discerning *the differences* in things. You can understand so you can prove and approve the more excellent things (see Philippians 1:9-10). That's understanding. The Spirit of God is "the spirit of wisdom and of understanding."

the spirit of counsel and might

Counsel is the ability to come to the right conclusion. That's counsel. Might is the energy to carry out the counsel. That's might. You need wisdom and understanding to begin with. Then you need counsel and might (strength) to put what you understand into practice, to bring it to realization.

the spirit of knowledge
and of the fear of Jehovah

And finally, the last pair, "the spirit of knowledge and of the fear of Jehovah." The "spirit of knowledge" is knowledge that is obtained through the fellowship of love. It is not just mental knowledge, but it is a knowledge that comes out of the fellowship of love. To know the Father and the One whom He sent—that is eternal life (see John 17:3). How do we know God? How do we know Him whom God has sent? It is through the fellowship of love that we come to a deep knowledge of God.

And this "fear of Jehovah" is not in contradiction with love. On the contrary, the more you love, the more you fear. You fear not because of punishment. You fear because you do not want to displease the One whom you love. So there is a reverence, a holy awe, that will be produced within that person.

This is the seven-fold Spirit:

> and (1) the Spirit of Jehovah shall rest upon him, (2) the spirit of wisdom (3) and understanding, (4) the spirit of

> counsel (5) and might, (6) the spirit of knowledge (7) and of the fear of Jehovah.

And this Spirit rested upon Christ. He is one with Christ. If you read the four Gospels, you will find this is how our Lord Jesus lived upon the earth. While He walked upon the earth, He was in the power of the Holy Spirit. There is an inspiration in Him; there is wisdom in Him, there is understanding in Him, there is counsel and might in Him, there is a knowledge of God and a fear of God in Him. You find our Lord Jesus exhibits the fullness of the Spirit, and that characterizes our Lord. What did He do? That is shared with us in verses 3-5:

> And his delight will be in the fear of Jehovah; and he shall not judge after the sight of his eyes, neither reprove after the hearing of his ears; but with righteousness shall he judge the poor, and reprove with equity the meek of the earth: and he shall smite the earth with the rod of his mouth, and with the breath of his lips shall he slay the wicked. And righteousness shall be the girdle of his reins, and faithfulness the girdle of his loins.

And his delight will be in the fear of Jehovah

The word here translated as *delight* is the word scent or smell in the original language (see Genesis 8:21; 27:27; Psalm 115:6). When the translators translated this, they just couldn't understand it. They just couldn't use the word *scent* and say: "his scent will be in the fear of Jehovah." They just couldn't make sense of that. And because of that, they translated it as *delight* instead. But, in the original, it is "his scent shall be in the fear of Jehovah; and he shall not judge after the sight of his eyes, neither reprove after the hearing of his ears."

Here you find three things: sight, hearing, and smell. The Lord Jesus will not judge after the seeing of His eyes, He will not reprove after the hearing of His ears, but His judgment will be based upon His smelling.

Now, you know smelling is more subtle and far-reaching than seeing and hearing. How far can you see? How far can you hear? If we are all in the same room, then we can see each other. But suppose one is behind a partition. Then though we cannot see, we can still hear if a baby cries. But scent or smell is more far-reaching and subtle than seeing and hearing.

I have some kind of a reaction against fish. If I go somewhere and someone is cooking fish—even if I were a far way out, outside of the door, outside of the house—as I approach the door, I smell fish. I don't see it, I don't hear it, but I smell it. Scent is a very subtle thing.

And when you come to the life of our Lord Jesus, as God's reaction, you will find that He judges not by hearing, not by seeing, but by His sense of smell. The Lord never judges anyone just by sight. He never judges anyone by what He hears from them. No, He judges by His scent, His smelling. This is spiritual discernment. This is an inward ability. It is not based upon appearance. Our Lord Jesus has a special sense of smell. He knows without seeing you or without hearing a word from you, He knows exactly what you are, where you are, where you stand. And He judges by that. That's scent—spiritual discernment.

And his [scent] will be in the fear of Jehovah

Where does this scent come from? How do you develop this scent?—in the fear of Jehovah. This "scent" is based on the fear of Jehovah. Brothers and sisters, our Lord Jesus never needs you to tell Him anything. He never needs to see anything in you. He knows you. He has that spiritual nose. He smells something in you. And as He smells, He judges. Therefore, His judgment is always true. He does not deal with you by what you appear to be. He never deals with you by what people say about you. No, He will judge by His scent. The Lord Jesus said that His judgment is true. Why? His judgment is righteous. Why? Because He does not judge according to himself, but He judges according to the One who has sent Him. And for the glory of the One who has sent Him. Therefore His judgment is always accurate and true (see John 8:16).

As you grow in the Lord, as you grow in the fear of the Lord, your scent will also grow with you. In II Corinthians, Paul said:

> For the love of the Christ constrains us, having judged this: that one died for all, then all have died; and he died for all, that they who live should no longer live to themselves, but to him who died for them and has been raised. So that we henceforth know no one according to flesh; but if even we have known Christ according to flesh, yet now we know him thus no longer (5:14-16).

Brothers and sisters, we know each other after the flesh. In other words, we know each other by hearing and seeing. I know you by seeing what you are and what you do. I know you by hearing what you say or what others say about you. We know each other after the flesh. And what a mistake Paul made with Christ. When he judged Christ after the flesh, he judged Christ as an imposter, as one who deserved to be persecuted. And he persecuted the followers of Christ from Jerusalem even to Gentile cities. But when Christ met him on the road to Damascus, his eyes were blind, and yet his scent was initiated. He said, "I no longer know Christ after the flesh; I know Him in spirit." And because of that, he knows nobody after the flesh, but he knows everybody according to the spirit.

Paul, following the way of Christ, knew no one after the flesh; he knew people in the spirit. And since he had that spiritual discernment, he was able to minister to people's needs. Spiritual discernment is necessary for ministry. Spiritual discernment is not for criticism. Spiritual discernment is not even for ordinary fellowship. Spiritual discernment is for ministry.

You know, there is a problem. The more you know, the less you are able to fellowship. Why? You know people too well to fellowship. The more you know, the more you are tempted to criticize. Why? Because you know so much. But dear brothers and sisters, fellowship is based on love, not on discernment. In order to have fellowship, sometimes you have to close your eyes. It is based on love. But ministry must be based on discernment. If you do not have that sense of smell, you cannot minister. Why? Because when people are hungry, you think they are full. When people are full, you think they are hungry. If you cannot smell, you do not know the real situation. Spiritual discernment is necessary for ministry.

In a sense, we all have that sense of smell built into us. Anyone who is born of the Lord has a little sense of smell in him. In I John 2, when John wrote to the little children, he said, "Little children the spirit of antichrist is in this world, but you know … you know. Even if your knowledge is very limited." The spirit of the antichrist is already in the world. How can you be kept from the spirit of the antichrist? How can you be kept from it? He said, "there is the anointing within you. And the anointing within you will keep you and teach you." Is that not true? Sometimes you go to hear a person. He may preach the word of God with great eloquence, or he may preach the word of God with lots of truth in it, but when you listen to a person, somehow, you smell something. You cannot put your finger on it. You do not know what it is because you do not have the knowledge. But you do smell that something is not quite right. There is something in that person. There is something in what he says. It looks all right, appears all right, and yet it is not right. You sense something within you. Brothers and sisters, that is scent. And that scent is in the fear of the Lord. Even with little children, this will keep them from hurt and harm.

the fear of Jehovah

This spiritual scent needs to be developed. And how is this to be developed?—in the fear of the Lord. The more you live in the fear of the Lord, the more the spiritual scent will be developed. And as the spiritual scent is developed, you are able to judge, and you are able to minister.

... but with righteousness shall he judge

Our Lord Jesus' scent will be in the fear of Jehovah, and He shall judge the poor and the meek.

> ... but with righteousness shall he judge the poor, and reprove with equity the meek of the earth: and he shall smite the earth with the rod of his mouth, and with the breath of his lips shall he slay the wicked. And righteousness shall be the girdle of his reins, and faithfulness the girdle of his loins.

Who are the poor and the meek? The poor and the meek are those who are redeemed by the Lord. So far as the world is concerned, they are the poor and the meek, but the Lord has judged them with equity. The Lord shall punish the wicked. Why?

> Righteousness shall be the girdle of his reins, and faithfulness the girdle of his loins.

Here is a problem. The judgment of the Lord is often beyond our understanding. You probably think: Now, if the Lord is to judge the poor and the meek and also the wicked, why is it that the poor and the meek suffer while the wicked seem to prosper? Where is the judgment of the Lord? How does He judge? Does He know how to judge? Has He judged rightly?

We often have such questions. If you are poor, you find you are oppressed. If you are meek, you find you are deprived. If you are wicked, you find that you prosper! Where is the Lord? Where is His judgment? Where is His righteousness? Where is His faithfulness?

> Blessed the meek, for they shall inherit the earth (Matthew 5:5).

Ah, if you are meek, certainly, you will lose the earth. Suppose you are very meek, and you have a piece of property. Your next-door neighbor begins to extend his house onto your property. Since you are meek, you will *lose* the earth. Yet the Bible says, "Blessed the meek for they shall *inherit* the earth." What does it mean by that? The judgment of the Lord is beyond our understanding.

There is a passage in II Thessalonians 1 that will probably explain it a little bit. The young church in Thessalonica was greatly persecuted. They suffered a great deal. Paul wrote this letter to comfort them.

> ... we ourselves make our boast in you in the assemblies of God for your endurance and faith in all your persecutions and tribulations, which ye are sustaining; a manifest token of the righteous judgment of God (vv. 4-5a).

Think about it! They were being persecuted, currently in tribulation, and Paul said this was "a manifest token of the righteous judgment of God"! Why did they suffer? Was it because they did something wrong? No. It was because they did something right! They did something right, and yet they were persecuted; they were in tribulation. Paul said, "this is a manifest token of the righteous judgment of God" that you are persecuted. Can we understand this?

> ... to the end that ye should be counted worthy of the kingdom of God, for the sake of which ye also suffer (v. 5b).

By all appearances, those who loved the Lord were persecuted and suffering, yet Paul said this was the manifest token of the righteous judgment of God. How? They were counted *worthy* of being persecuted and suffer for the kingdom of God. They were given grace for endurance and faith. This is the manifest token of the righteous judgment of God.

In other words, the kingdom of God is in view. Oftentimes we look at things just for the present time. If you see judgment only for the present time, then you'll find the whole scene is distorted. The righteous seem to suffer; the wicked seem to prosper. But if you can see far enough ahead, the Lord is judging. The Lord is judging those who are righteous. They suffer that they may be counted worthy of the kingdom of God. Your suffering is for the kingdom of God. If you do not suffer, you cannot enter into the kingdom of God. If you are not willing to suffer, you are not qualified to enter into the kingdom of God. But while you suffer, you are given grace to endure; you are given faith to continue. This is God's judgment. Do you see the point?

> ... if at least it is a righteous thing with God to render tribulation to those that trouble you, and to you that are troubled repose with us, at the revelation of the Lord Jesus from heaven, with the angels of his power (vv. 6-7).

It is true that today the wicked seem to prosper, but their prosperity is the righteous judgment of God. God permits them to prosper so that they may be ready for the time of slaughter. Just like you feed a hog. You let the hog prosper; you feed the hog. Why? For the day of slaughtering. That is God's judgment.

Oh, brothers and sisters, that is the way the Lord judges! And that's why it always is beyond us. Oftentimes we misunderstand Him. Oh, if only we can see what is in view! If only we can see the end, then we will find His judgment is righteous, and His judgment is faithful. We will realize that He is dealing faithfully and righteously with us, and we will not misunderstand Him. Why? Because He judges by His scent. He is not wrong at all. He is right.

the earth shall be full of the knowledge of Jehovah

What will the ultimate result be? What will the consummation be? The Lord is judging. The Lord has been and is still judging all these days. Even today, the Lord is judging. He is judging with equity. He is judging with righteousness and faithfulness. Even though we may not see it to be so, yet He is. Do you know what will happen ultimately? At the very end? After He judges, and judges, He will bring in His kingdom. At the very end, you find the kingdom of God shall come upon this earth, and this is the way it should come.

The spiritual reality must be here first before there can be the physical manifestation of the kingdom of God. Do you think that the kingdom of God will suddenly drop out of heaven upon the earth? Not so. The kingdom of God will come upon this earth because the Lord has been preparing the ground throughout these twenty centuries. The Lord is judging. The Lord is preparing His people. The Lord is bringing in the reality of the kingdom. The spirit of the kingdom shall fill this earth first. There shall be a people who are filled with the spirit of the kingdom, and when this has arrived, then the kingdom of God shall publicly be manifested upon this earth. This is the millennium kingdom that lasts for a thousand years:

> The wolf also shall dwell with the lamb, and the leopard shall lie down with the kid, and the calf and the young lion and the fatted beast together, and a little child shall lead them. And the cow and the she-bear shall feed; their young ones shall lie down together; and the lion shall eat straw like the ox. And the sucking child shall play on the hole of the adder, and the weaned child shall put forth its hand to the viper's den (Isaiah 11:6-8).

Here is a description of the kingdom of God on earth. The curse of sin has been removed. God has restored everything—the whole creation—to His original design. General restitution has come upon this earth. Not only will a lion not attack an ox, but a lion will eat straw like an ox. The very nature, the carnivorous nature of a lion, will change. He will no longer be a meat-eating animal. He will become a vegetarian eating grass. The very nature of things will change.

That old nature was there in the Garden of Eden. In the coming kingdom, there will be a reversal of the curse of the fall of man. Before man fell, in the Garden of Eden, all these animals lived together in peace with man. But the sin of man changed the nature of everything. It changed the nature of man to now be the Adamic sinful nature. It changed the nature of the animals. It changed the nature of grass and everything. That was the curse. But here through Christ, the redemption of Christ reaches not only to man but to the whole creation. The whole creation has been redeemed and restored to its original state. The nature of creation has changed and transformed back. Why? The reason is:

> They shall not hurt nor destroy in all my holy mountain; for the earth shall be full of the knowledge of Jehovah, as the waters cover the sea (v.9).

When the knowledge of the Lord shall fill the earth as the waters cover the sea, then nothing hurts or destroys. It is the knowledge of the Lord. Brothers and sisters, how important is the knowledge of the Lord. Oh, how important that we know Him! Why? Because to know Him is not just to know something in our minds, making our brains big, as it were. No. Knowing the Lord will transform us. What is the power of transformation? The knowledge of the Lord. Why is this world the way that we see it today? It is due to the lack of the knowledge of the Lord. When the knowledge of the Lord shall fill the earth, as waters fill the sea, then "they shall not hurt nor destroy" anything.

There shall be a root of Jesse,
standing as a banner of the peoples

Oh, brothers and sisters, how we look forward to that day when the kingdom of God shall come upon this earth! How will the kingdom of God come upon this earth? Through Christ. He is God's reaction! Through Christ, He brings in His judgment. He brings in the kingdom upon this earth. And He shall be as a banner, and all the nations shall flow to

Him. This is the beautiful picture of the consummation of God's reaction to this world through one person—Christ.

So dear brothers and sisters, do remember this: the principle of God's reaction is Christ. If we allow Christ to judge us, if we learn to submit ourselves under His mighty hand, then in due time, He will exalt us. To Him be all the praise and the glory.

4—In Returning and Rest

Isaiah 30:15-21—For thus saith the Lord Jehovah, the Holy One of Israel: In returning and rest shall ye be saved, in quietness and confidence shall be your strength; but ye would not. And ye said, No, but we will flee upon horses, —therefore shall ye flee; and, We will ride upon the swift, —therefore shall they that pursue you be swift. One thousand shall flee at the rebuke of one; at the rebuke of five shall ye flee: till ye be left as a beacon upon the top of a mountain, and as a banner on a hill. And therefore will Jehovah wait, that he may be gracious unto you, and therefore will he lift himself up, that he may have mercy upon you; for Jehovah is a God of judgment: blessed are all they that wait for him. For the people shall dwell in Zion, at Jerusalem. Thou shalt weep no more; he will be very gracious unto thee at the voice of thy cry; as he heareth it, he will answer thee. And the Lord will give you the bread of adversity, and the water of oppression; yet thy teachers shall not be hidden any more, but thine eyes shall see thy teachers. And when ye turn to the right hand or when ye turn to the left, thine ears shall hear a word behind thee, saying, This is the way, walk ye in it.

In order to understand this passage of the Scripture, I think we must know a little bit about the background.

Judah's Situation

The nation of Judah was situated at that time between two great nations. On the North was the kingdom of Assyria, and in the South was the kingdom of Egypt. This little nation of Judah was squeezed, as it were, between these two great nations. Whenever there was a campaign, Assyria would pass through the land of Judah to reach Egypt, and vice versa. Judah was in a very difficult situation. And as a little nation, she had to try to balance herself between these two powers. Humanly speaking, Judah had to be very clever, walking a tightrope, trying to balance one superpower against the other for her own survival. And this was what she did. Whenever Judah was in trouble from one nation, she tried to seek the help of the other nation, and vice versa.

This balancing act is probably what happened at the time of King Hezekiah. We know that King Hezekiah was a good king, and yet he was faced with such a dilemma. In order to fight against the oppression of Assyria, he sought the help of Egypt (see II Kings 18). But while King Hezekiah was doing that, the word of God came through the prophet Isaiah. Why? Because instead of going to the Lord for help, instead of seeking the Lord's face, the little nation of Judah was trying to solve their dilemma by their own wisdom, by their own cleverness. This was considered as rebellion against the Lord. A nation that was supposed to know the Lord forgot their God and tried to seek the help of an earthly kingdom. God was not pleased with that. So He sent His prophet Isaiah to the nation and said, "If you seek the help of Egypt, you will find that Egypt is like a broken reed. Both you and Egypt will fall."

The word of the Lord to the nation of Judah at that specific time was this:

> In returning and rest shall ye be saved. In quietness and confidence shall be your strength.

What they needed to do was to *return* to God and *rest* in God—then they would *be saved. In quietness* (not in running around) *and confidence* (not in man, but in God)—*shall be [their] strength.* This was the word of God to that little nation of Judah at that time.

The Church's Situation

Now let us apply this word to us today. The church of God is a "little flock" compared to this world:

> Fear not, little flock, for it has been the good pleasure of your Father to give you the kingdom (Luke 12:32).

And, in a sense, this little flock is situated between two great forces. On the one side is the secular world—represented by Egypt; on the other side is the religious world—represented by Assyria or Babylon. God has delivered us out of the world—out of Egypt as with the Israelites—but we find ourselves oppressed by the religious world—Babylon and Assyria. Then, to balance against the oppression that comes from the religious world, we seek the help of the secular world and vice versa.

Let me illustrate this with what happened at the time of the Reformation in the 16th century. At that time, the reformers were raised up by God to seek deliverance from the papacy—the Pope and the Roman Catholic religious system.

Yet, while doing so, they received the help of earthly princes. The result was that sometimes the church of God was under the oppression of the secular world, and the other times she was captured by the religious world. The word of God to His people is:

> In returning and rest shall ye be saved, in quietness and confidence shall be your strength

The Believer's Situation

Now let us apply this same principle to us as individuals. We often find ourselves surrounded by adverse forces. Suppose we are placed in a situation where we are pressed from all sides; what are we going to do to get out of it? We may have lots of problems, coming from all directions—what are we going to do? Our natural tendency when we are pressed is to make a plan. We try to figure out a way out. We try to seek help from one side in order to balance out the other side. When we are in times of trouble, when we are under pressure, when we have trials, our first reaction will be to try to figure a way out. Try to balance these forces; try to solve them with our cleverness. And when we are doing that, we find ourselves running hither and thither, we struggle and strive, we worry, we complain, we doubt, we lose our sleep and get restless. We forget to return to the Lord. We have a God who is faithful, and yet when we are met with practical problems, we forget we have a God. Our reaction typically is all from ourselves—looking to man for help. What rebellious people we are. The word of God to us is to return. Return and rest!—then we shall be saved. How we need to return to the Lord again and again!

The Way of Deliverance

In returning and rest shall ye be saved ...

Sometimes in the Scripture, you find such prayers as "Lord turn to us and we will turn to Thee" as if the Lord needs to return to us! (see Lamentations 5:21) So far as our feeling is concerned, sometimes we feel that God has left us, He has forsaken us, and we cry out that He should turn back to us, He should return to us, and then we will return to Him. Now, this is our *feeling*. But so far as the *fact* is concerned, He has not left us nor has He forsaken us (see Hebrews 13:5). It is we who have left *Him*! We should return to Him. And if we return, we will find that He is already waiting there for us.

Of course, the power to return has to come from Him, that's true. But thank God, He is always here. He has never left us nor forsaken us. He is waiting for us to return to Him. We need to return to Him. And as we return to Him, then we rest in His finished work. We rest in all that He has promised us. The Lord Jesus said:

> Come to me, all ye who labour and are burdened, and I will give you rest. Take my yoke upon you, and learn from me; for I am meek and lowly in heart; and ye shall find rest to your souls (Matthew 11:28-29).

We need to come to the Lord. We need to return to the Lord. Whenever we are pressed, brothers and sisters, the first thing to do is to return to Him. And as we return to the Lord, we shall find rest. We begin to see all that He is, what He has accomplished for us, who He is, what He has promised. As we start to see these things, we are resting. There is no need to doubt; there is no need to worry; there is no need to struggle or to fret. We just return and rest. Once we come to Him and rest in Him, we will be saved. We "shall be saved"!

in quietness and confidence shall be your strength

There is more to this than just to be saved—in quietness and confidence shall be your strength! To be saved is one thing, but to be strong is another. He will not only save us if we return and rest in Him but as we return and learn to rest in Him, we also enter into a quietness—our flesh begins to be calmed.

When we are not quiet but are restless, we waste a lot of our energy and strength as we struggle and strive. Oh, if only we can return to Him and see Him!

> Let all flesh be silent before Jehovah; for he is risen up out of his holy habitation (Zechariah 2:13).

The Lord is in His sanctuary; let all flesh be quiet. If we enter behind the veil, in the holiest of all, everything is quiet. This is a life behind the veil. It is a life with the Lord. As we enter behind the veil, everything is suddenly quiet. Then we see the Lord, and confidence begins to rise up in us. We know He is trustworthy. Paul said that our confidence is not in ourselves but God (see II Corinthians 1:9). Our confidence is in Him.

God has a word for us today. He is calling us to return and rest in Him, for this shall be our salvation. He is calling us to enter into quietness and confidence, and we shall find spiritual strength for our everyday need.

but ye would not

> ... but ye would not. And ye said, No, but we will flee upon horses, —therefore shall ye flee; and, We will ride upon the swift, —therefore shall they that pursue you be swift. One thousand shall flee at the rebuke of one; at the rebuke of five shall ye flee: till ye be left as a beacon upon the top of a mountain, and as a banner on a hill (Isaiah 30:15d-17).

Did the nation of Israel receive that word? No. They said, "We will not. We will run, we will be swift." In other words, they wanted to rely on something tangible and visible. They did not have faith to believe in the God who is invisible, who seems to be intangible to their flesh. They would rather rely on something that they could lay hold on with their hands. They would not listen to God, they would not return to the Lord, and the result was that God said, "All right, if you want to run, you will run. If you want to be swift, you will be *pursued* with swiftness. At the rebuke of one, a thousand will flee; at the rebuke of five, all of you will flee."

Now think of this—what a reversal of the promise of God! In the past, God had said, "If you keep my statutes, my commandments, then one will make a hundred flee, and a hundred will make ten thousand flee. But if you do not listen to My word, then ye will flee even without anyone pursuing" (see Leviticus 26:1,7-8, 14, 17). The nation of Israel did not listen to God, so at the rebuke of one, a thousand started to flee, and at the rebuke of five, all were fleeing. In other words, they were put under the disciplining hands of God.

Dear brothers and sisters, what should be our attitude before God? Life is full of pressure. Life is full of problems. What should be our reaction? What should be our attitude? "In returning and rest shall be your salvation, in quietness and confidence shall be your strength."

And if we do not, what will be the result? We will be under the disciplinary hand of God.

And therefore will Jehovah wait,
that he may be gracious

Do you think that since we forsake the Lord that God will forsake us? Not so. In verse 18, we read, "therefore will Jehovah wait, that He may be gracious unto you." The Lord has not left us nor forsaken us. He is there patiently waiting for us that He may be gracious to us. He wants to be gracious to us, but He cannot. He wants to "lift himself up, that he may have mercy upon [us]," but He cannot. He has to wait for us until we are ready. Do you think that we are waiting for God? No, He is waiting for us.

And therefore will Jehovah wait
... blessed are all they that wait for him

> And therefore will Jehovah wait, that he may be gracious unto you, and therefore will he lift himself up, that he may have mercy upon you; for Jehovah is a God of judgment: blessed are all they that wait for him (Isaiah 30:18).

Here are two waitings. First, God is waiting for us so that He may be merciful and gracious. And second, those who wait upon the Lord are blessed. He waits for us until we wait for Him.

In one of brother Watchman Nee's books, he mentioned his experience that illustrates this principle. Once, he and a few others went swimming, and one of them began to sink! He was drowning. Brother Nee himself was not a good swimmer, but there was a good swimmer there. So he expected that brother to jump in and rescue the drowning one. But instead, that brother who was good at swimming just stood there and watched.

Brother Nee got so worried and excited and said, "Now why don't you swim and rescue him!?! Why is your heart so hard? You see that this brother is sinking and drowning, and you stand there and watch! How can you do that!?!"

But that brother wouldn't do anything. He just stood there and watched, letting the drowning man sink down and float back up and sink down again. Finally, when the drowning brother came up the third time and was sinking the third time, that brother who could swim jumped into the water and brought him to the shore.

Brother Nee couldn't understand, so afterward, he asked that brother, "Why did you do such a thing? You could have saved him before he suffered so long. Why didn't you do it?"

And that brother said, "You don't know how this works. If a man is sinking and someone tries to rescue him, he will cling to that man uncontrollably, and both will go down in the water. You have to let him give up everything until he no longer struggles—as if dead—then you can bring him to the shore."

How true this is with us! How often we misunderstand God and say, "Lord, we are in trouble! We are sinking! We are drowning! We don't know what to do. We are running hither and thither. We have tried everything we can, and it doesn't seem to help. Now, where are you? Do you really care? Why do you stand by and just watch and do nothing!?!"

How often we murmur against God, not knowing that we are under discipline, not knowing that He cannot do anything. Why can't He do anything? Because we are still struggling. We do not return to Him! We do not rest! There is no quietness. There is no confidence. He has to allow us to get to the end of ourselves. Once we come to the end of ourselves and say, "Well, this is it. I am finished," is it finished? No. That is only the beginning. You discover that God is waiting for you. He is waiting there until you give up every struggle and strife—until you enter into rest. Then He will be gracious to you. He will lift himself up and rescue you.

Dear brothers and sisters, we will not wait upon the Lord until we consider ourselves dead. If there is anything still alive there, we want to rescue ourselves. We want to try. Blessed are they that wait upon Him. When you come to the point of waiting upon the Lord, you find that the Lord is waiting there for you. He has been waiting there the whole time. He has not forsaken you. He has heard you. When you cried, He heard you.

... the bread of adversity,
and the water of oppression ...

> And the Lord will give you the bread of adversity, and the water of oppression; yet thy teachers shall not be hidden any more, but thine eyes shall see thy teachers. And when ye turn to the right hand or when ye turn to

> the left, thine ears shall hear a word behind thee, saying, This is the way, walk ye in it. (Isaiah 30:20-21)

Though He heard you, He still gave you the bread of adversity and the water of oppression. That's true. Who likes adversity? But God gives you the *bread* of adversity. We all like bread, but we don't like adversity. We all want water, but we do not want oppression. But God gives us the *water* of oppression. In other words, oppression and adversity are bread and water for us. They will feed us. They will satisfy us. Since God is there with us, even adversity and oppression are bread and water for us to eat and drink.

When God gives us the bread of adversity and the water of oppression, our "teachers shall not be hidden." Adversity and oppression are good teachers. If the Spirit of God is in them, they are good teachers. Sometimes we are so stubborn that we have to learn the hard way. Oh, if only we are meek and lowly in heart; if only we would listen and not harden our hearts; if only we would return and rest; if only we would enter into quietness and confidence—but we will not. We have to learn the hard way. God has to give us the bread of adversity and the water of oppression in order to teach us. Then, if we "turn to the right hand or … to the left," the word comes to us: "This is the way, walk ye in it." What is the way? The way is, "In returning and rest shall ye be saved, in quietness and confidence shall be your strength." That is the way.

The Result of Returning and Resting

Do you know what the result or outcome is? God delivered them from idols and anything foreign to himself:

> And ye shall defile the silver covering of your graven images, and the gold overlaying of your molten images; thou shalt cast them away ... (Isaiah 30:22)

And God gave them rain, seed, abundance, and water:

> And he will give the rain of thy seed with which thou shalt sow the ground; and bread, the produce of the ground, and it shall be fat and rich. In that day shall thy cattle feed in large pastures; and the oxen and the asses that till the ground shall eat salted provender, which hath been winnowed with the shovel and with the fan. And there shall be upon every high mountain and upon every hill that is lifted up, brooks and water-courses, in the day of the great slaughter, when the towers fall (vv. 23-25).

And the moon shall shine as the sun, and the sun shall shine seven-fold:

> And the light of the moon shall be as the light of the sun, and the light of the sun shall be sevenfold, as the light of seven days, in the day that Jehovah bindeth up the breach of his people, and healeth the wound of their stroke (v. 26).

In other words, through all these troubles, God is teaching us; and after we are taught, we will enter into the riches of Christ.

So dear brothers and sisters, I believe God wants us to have this word, meditate upon it, take it to heart, and practice it by the grace of God. Whenever you are having a problem, whenever you are in trouble, whenever you are under pressure, remember this:

> In returning and rest shall ye be saved, in quietness and confidence shall be your strength.

5—Comfort Ye, Comfort Ye My People

Isaiah 40:1-5, 31—Comfort ye, comfort ye my people, saith your God. Speak to the heart of Jerusalem, and cry unto her, that her time of suffering is accomplished, that her iniquity is pardoned; for she hath received of Jehovah's hand double for all her sins. The voice of one crying in the wilderness: Prepare ye the way of Jehovah, make straight in the desert a highway for our God! Every valley shall be raised up, and every mountain and hill shall be brought low; and the crooked shall be made straight, and the rough places a plain. And the glory of Jehovah shall be revealed, and all flesh shall see it together: for the mouth of Jehovah hath spoken. ... but they that wait upon Jehovah shall renew their strength: they shall mount up with wings as eagles; they shall run, and not tire; they shall walk, and not faint.

The book of Isaiah can be very roughly divided into two parts: 1) In chapters 1-39, the prophet is more concerned with history; 2) and in chapters 40-66, the prophet Isaiah is distinctly concerned with prophecy. The theme of this second part agrees with the meaning of the name of the prophet—Isaiah means *the salvation of the LORD*. This second part deals mainly with the salvation of the Lord. It tells us of the work of redemption of our Lord. It tells us of our Redeemer. It tells us of those that are redeemed. It is altogether concerned with this matter of salvation, of redemption, of deliverance that comes from the Lord. And it begins with a cry. It is the cry of the Lord through the prophet to His people: "Comfort ye, comfort ye my people" (Isaiah 40:1).

Due to the unfaithfulness of the children of Israel, they were chastened by the Lord. And the chastening was of such nature that they were even taken into captivity. But the Lord returned to them in mercy and in grace. And the word of the Lord to His afflicted people was, "Comfort ye, comfort ye my people." God considered their punishment as enough. God had forgiven their iniquities. And God was now returning to His people. God said, "Be ye comforted." Now dear brothers and sisters, I believe we all need to be comforted.

This word *comfort*, when used in the Greek* language, simply means "calling to one's side." That is to say, to come to your aid, to exhort you, to encourage you, and to comfort you. It can even mean to strengthen you. These are the various meanings of the word *comfort* in Greek. And when it refers to a person, it is the Comforter—*parakletos* (e.g., John 14:26). A *comforter* is one who is called to your side to take up your cause, to plead for you, and to render you every help that you need.

> Blessed be the God and Father of our Lord Jesus Christ, the Father of compassions, and God of all encouragement [or, "comfort" KJV]; who encourages [comforts] us in all our tribulation, that we may be able to encourage [comfort] those who are in any tribulation whatever, through the encouragement [comfort] with

*While Isaiah 40:1 was originally written in Hebrew, the author uses the LXX translation of Isaiah 40:1 to obtain the Greek word for comfort—*parakaleo*. By obtaining the Greek equivalent to the Hebrew original, *nacham*, he then compares it with New Testament usages. –*Transcriber*

> which we ourselves are encouraged [comforted] of God. (II Corinthians 1:3).

The Triune God of All Comfort

Our God is the God of all comfort. First of all, God, our Father, is the "Father of compassions." He is full of compassion, the *Father* of compassion, the God of all comfort. Second, our Lord Jesus is "the consolation [or comfort] of Israel." In Luke chapter 2, Simeon was looking for the comfort of Israel; and this referred to our Lord Jesus (v. 25). And third, the Holy Spirit is the "another Comforter":

> And I will beg the Father, and he will give you **another Comforter**, that he may be with you for ever, the Spirit of truth, ... ye know him, for he abides with you, and shall be in you. I will not leave you orphans, I am coming to you (John 14:16-18).

Why is He called the "another Comforter"? Because our Lord Jesus was a Comforter to His disciples when He was with them. In John 14, as He was about to go away, He promised to send "another Comforter"—the Holy Spirit. This word *another* means *another of the same kind*. He shared how the Holy Spirit would be with them and in them and would never leave nor forsake them. The Holy Spirit was with the disciples forever to be their comfort, to be their Comforter.

So dear brothers and sisters, remember that our God is the God of all comfort. This word comfort is His very name. It speaks of His work and reveals His very nature. It is His wish to comfort us, to strengthen us.

The Comfort of Discipline

Sometimes He may have to discipline us, yet do not misunderstand Him. He has no desire just to punish us. Instead, He is the consolation; He is the comfort; He is the Comforter. We all need to be comforted. Sometimes because of our sins, our failures, and our unbelief, God has to chasten or discipline us. During the time of chastening, it is not a pleasant and joyful time. But even so, you find His rod comforts us.

> Yea, though I walk through the valley of the shadow of death, I will fear no evil: for thou art with me; thy rod and thy staff, they comfort me (Psalm 23:4).

Sometimes we enter into the valley of the shadow of death. Sometimes we may enter into His discipline. Yes, His *staff* comforts us. The staff is there to help, to rescue, and to lead. Certainly, His staff comforts us. But don't forget that His *rod* comforts us too! Though sometimes He may have to smite us, He may have to apply the rod upon us and make us still, yet still "Thy rod" comforts us. Why? Because He is the God of all comfort. The reason why He disciplines us is that He loves us. In the very fact of His rod, there is the expression of His love. If He did not care, if He did not love us, He would not even chasten us!

> ... for whom the Lord loves he chastens, and scourges every son whom he receives (Hebrews 12:6).

It is the rod of God's love, the rod of His comfort.

I remember reading somewhere in a book that once a youngster said his parents did not love him. Why? Because his parents never disciplined him, the rod was never applied to him. "Thy rod … comfort[s] me."

Tribulation to Comfort Others

Sometimes tribulation may not be because we have sinned or failed. For example, Paul in II Corinthians mentioned how God is the God of all comfort, how He encourages him, how He comforts him in all his tribulation. Now certainly, Paul went into tribulation not because he was unfaithful but because he was *too* faithful. Sometimes since you are faithful to the Lord, you will get into trouble and have problems. You may be persecuted or have tribulation. Why? Not because there is something negative in your life, but because God is working something positive into your life. In tribulation, you will be comforted that you may comfort those who shall be in tribulation. You will be comforted in order that the Lord may use you to minister to those who are in need. He allows you to go through tribulation and be encouraged and comforted that you may encourage and comfort those who are in need. That's positive.

> Blessed be the God and Father of our Lord Jesus Christ, the Father of compassions, and God of all [comfort]; who **[comforts] us in all our tribulation, that we may be able to [comfort] those who are in any tribulation** whatever, through the [comfort] with which we ourselves are [comforted] of God. Because, even as the sufferings of the Christ abound towards us, so through

> the Christ does our [comfort] also abound. **But whether we are in tribulation, it is for your [comfort]** and salvation, wrought in the endurance of the same sufferings which we also suffer, (and our hope for you is sure;) or **whether we are [comforted], it is for your [comfort]** and salvation: knowing that as ye are partakers of the sufferings, so also of the [comfort] (II Corinthians 1:3-7 emphasis added).

So dear brothers and sisters, our life is full of problems, our life is full of all kinds of circumstances. Sometimes because of our failure, we are disciplined. Other times it is that God wants to work something positive in us that we may be useful in His hand.

We All Need to Be Comforted

And when we are under all kinds of circumstances, do we need to be comforted? Is there anyone that does not have the need for comfort? Look at Paul. Why surely Paul is a spiritual giant! He is strong. But does he need to be comforted? When you read II Corinthians, you will find the word comfort is used 11 times. (I hope you go through it and find all the places where the words comfort or encourage or encouragement are used.) Even Paul needs comfort. How he was concerned with the conditions of the Corinthians! He sent Titus to them, and he made an agreement with Titus to meet him in Troas. But when Paul came to Troas, and Titus did not come back, Paul was so concerned that he could not work! The Lord had opened a door for him in Troas, and yet he could not work. He went on to Macedonia since Titus was late. Then when

Titus arrived, Paul was comforted by the very presence of Titus and also the glad tidings that Titus brought back. Paul needed to be comforted (2:12-13, 7:4-7).

There is no one who does not need, at one time or another, to be comforted. Some people probably need it more than other people, but how we all need to be comforted! And thank God He is the God of all comfort. It is His word to His afflicted people: "Comfort ye, comfort ye my people." The Lord desires to comfort us. The word comfort means more than just consolation; it means strengthening. God comforts us to strengthen us. This is our God.

God's Comfort—His Presence

Now how did God comfort His people? The nation of Israel was in captivity. How was God going to comfort them? In what way would God comfort His afflicted people? Was it by bringing them back to Jerusalem? Was it by turning their captivity? Remember, these were the outward circumstances. The real comfort that God used to comfort His afflicted people was the promise of the coming of the Messiah. In other words, the comfort of the Lord is His presence with His people. When He promises to come back, when He promises to be with His people—"Behold, thy King cometh. Behold the Lord is now with you."—when the Lord comes back to His people, then His afflicted people are comforted.

> O Zion, that bringest glad tidings, get thee up into a high mountain; O Jerusalem, that bringest glad tidings, lift up thy voice with strength: lift it up, be not afraid; say unto the cities of Judah, Behold your God! Behold, the Lord Jehovah will come with might, and his arm shall rule for

him; behold, his reward is with him, and his recompence before him (Isaiah 40:9-10).

In other words, comfort is not just changing your circumstances. Comfort is not just bringing you into a better position. All these things will happen, but remember, the real comfort that God comforts His people with is himself. He comforts us with His coming to us. Is there any comfort better than that?

Sometimes, especially when we are surrounded by problems and troubles, especially when we are under tribulation or discipline, we feel that the Lord has left us. We feel as if He has forsaken us. And oftentimes, the psalmist will cry out, "Why? Why do You leave us? Where are You? Why don't You speak? Why do you keep Your silence? Where can I find You?" (Psalms 10:1; 22:1; 28:1 42:9; 74:1) This agitation and turmoil spring up in our soul because we feel the Lord has left us, He has forsaken us, He has turned His back on us, He has been silent toward us—we cry, and He does not answer.

Now, brothers and sisters, it is often true, so far as our emotions are concerned, that when we find ourselves in such a situation, we don't allow ourselves to be comforted. No matter what people say, no matter how people say it, we just refuse to be comforted. Why? Because we feel the Lord has left us, the Lord has forsaken us. He has turned His back on us. That is our feeling. Oh, if only He will return to us! Then all these tribulations would not matter anymore.

What is the greatest hardship to a believer? It is not a difficult situation. It is the feeling of being forsaken. If the Lord is present with you, no matter how hard things may be, you are comforted, and there is strength! But when you feel the Lord has left you or forsaken you, then you are finished.

Think of our Lord Jesus. Throughout His life, the sense of the presence of His Father was ever with Him. No matter what happened to Him, there was that comfort within Him. Even when He was crucified on the cross, surrounded by His enemies—oh, how the people ridiculed Him! How Satan tried to use every means to hurt Him and to harm Him!—yet when He was on the cross, He could pray, "Father, forgive them, for they know not what they do" (Luke 23:34). His Father was with Him. There was strength! But then, as the sun was darkened, at the ninth hour our Lord Jesus began to cry out, "My God, My God, why hast Thou forsaken Me?" (Matthew 27:46) The very presence of His Father had left Him. He was all alone as a sin offering for the whole world, and He couldn't stand it. He cried out in desperation. Now that is the hardest thing for a believer.

Oh, sometimes you may feel or think that God has left you. You may think that you are alone, and so you completely collapse. You do not know what to do. You need to be comforted. And how are you to be comforted? By the return of the Lord. If only He will come back to you, then you do not mind what circumstances you may be in. Those are not the problem. You will have the strength to bear it. His coming to you is your comfort.

But has He ever left you or forsaken you? So far as your feeling is concerned, it may be true that He has left you. But dear brothers and sisters, you know that He has never left you nor forsaken you (see Hebrews 13:5). He is waiting to appear to you. And the reason why it seems there is a veil or covering is that He wants to teach you some lessons.

Oh, how the Lord himself is our Comforter! There is no one who can comfort us except our Lord Jesus. He is our consolation. And His being with us is our strength.

Preparing the Way for Comfort to Come

God spoke to the children of Israel, "Comfort ye, comfort ye my people." But how did the comfort come to them? There was a process. Immediately after the cry of "comfort," there was a cry in the wilderness:

> The voice of one crying in the wilderness: Prepare ye the way of Jehovah, make straight in the desert a highway for our God! Every valley shall be raised up, and every mountain and hill shall be brought low; and the crooked shall be made straight, and the rough places a plain (Isaiah 40:3-4).

Historically we know that this prophecy was fulfilled with the coming of John the Baptist. John the Baptist was the voice in the wilderness. John the Baptist was sent before the coming of Christ to prepare the way for the Lord—a *highway* for the Lord (see Mark 1:1-4).

Sometimes God cannot reach you. God wants to reach you, but there is no way, no path. Sometimes we are like a desert. There are valleys and mountains, crooked and rough places in our lives. And the Lord cannot reach us. There is no highway for God to come to us. Because of this, certain preparation is necessary.

Before Christ could come to the nation of Israel, John the Baptist must first be sent as a forerunner to prepare the way of the Lord. He prepared the way by calling the people to repent: "Repent, for the kingdom of heaven is at hand" (Matthew 3:2 NKJV). The nation needed to repent *before* they were ready to receive the Messiah, the Christ.

In principle, this is also true with us today. God is the God of all comfort. It is His wish to comfort us and to strengthen us. But sometimes He has no way to reach us. It is not that He does not want to comfort us. We think that we need comfort, and He keeps delaying. Not so. The delay is because there is no preparation of the heart.

There are valleys in our lives—hidden, secret, sins, weaknesses—low places like valleys there. Sometimes there are mountains and hills in our lives—unbelief, vanity, pride. These are like mountains standing in the way. Sometimes there is crookedness; other times, there is roughness. The "crooked and rough" description reminds me of two brothers—Esau and Jacob. Jacob was crooked, and Esau was rough. We have both Esau and Jacob within us. There is that crooked Jacob in us, not straight. And there is the rough Esau in us.

These valleys need to be raised and filled, the mountains needed to be leveled, the crooked paths need to be made straight, and these rough places need to be made smooth. Brothers and sisters, this is the needed preparation.

How often we desire to be comforted, we long to be comforted, we are waiting to be comforted. But all the while the Spirit of God is working in us with the ministry of John the Baptist. In other words, the Spirit of God is convicting us and bringing us into repentance. He is dealing with the crookedness and the roughness of our lives. He is dealing with the hills and the mountains and the valleys of our lives. And unless the hidden valleys are raised and exposed, our mountains are removed, our crookedness made straight, and our roughness made smooth, He has no highway to reach us.

Thank God, He is faithful. He *is* coming to us, but there must be repentance. We must accept the convicting and convincing work of the Holy Spirit in us. We must allow Him to deal with us until we are ready for the King—ready to receive Him as our King as our Shepherd. And truly, He will come as a Shepherd to us; He will take us in His arms, He will carry us (see Isaiah 40:11). He is the Comforter.

The comfort will come, but it has to come by way of the ministry of John the Baptist. Because unless it comes that way, we are not ready.

Wait Upon Him

When we are discouraged, we are discouraged. We want to be comforted, and yet we do not want to be comforted. So God said:

> Why sayest thou, Jacob, and speakest, O Israel, My way is hid from Jehovah, and my right is passed away from my God? (Isaiah 40:27).

Even though God spoke the word of comfort to His people, His people did not believe it. His people said, "My way is hid from Jehovah, and my right is passed away from my God. God just does not care. And if He does care, what can He do?" They forget that our God is the God who:

> ... measured the waters in the hollow of his hand, and meted out the heavens with his span, and grasped the dust

> of the earth in a measure, and weighed the mountains in a balance, and the hills in scales (v. 12).

Beautiful. Wonderful. Think of it: He measured waters in the hollow of His hand! There is just the right amount of water in this world. If there were too much water, the earth would be overwhelmed, drowned. God *measured* the water in the hollow of His hand. He meted out the heavens with His span. How wide, how big is heaven? We are lost with astronomical figures. And God measured the heavens with His span. Everything is measured. He grabbed the dust of the earth in a measure. He weighed the mountains in the balance. Everything is balanced. There is no weakness in Him—both in His power and in His love. And yet, brothers and sisters, sometimes we can get so discouraged. All we see is our problems. We want to be comforted, yet we refuse to be comforted. And we say, "No. It doesn't work. It won't do. God doesn't care. He cannot do anything with me. I am just finished." God said, "Why? Why do you say this?"

> Dost thou not know, hast thou not heard, that the everlasting God, Jehovah, the Creator of the ends of the earth, fainteth not nor tireth? There is no searching of his understanding (v.28).

Have you forgotten who God is? Don't you remember that His understanding is so great, and He knows everything? The exhortation of the Lord to those who are so discouraged is:

> ... but they that wait upon Jehovah shall renew their strength: they shall mount up with wings as eagles; they shall run, and not tire; they shall walk, and not faint (v. 31).

If you are in need of comfort and yet you are not comforted, if you are discouraged to the point of despair, remember this: God said for you to wait upon Him. He is waiting there for you, but He exhorts you to wait upon Him. He is coming to you if you just wait upon Him.

In the Scripture, the word *wait* does not mean sitting back passively. No, that's not waiting. To wait is an active-passive waiting. It is true that by waiting, you do not struggle or strive, and yet by waiting, you also wait with expectancy. You are still before the Lord, and yet you are waiting upon Him with expectancy, with belief, with faith.

If you wait upon the Lord, what will be the result? You will "mount up with wings as eagles." Some people who know about eagles tell us that when eagles fly, they do not need to flap their wings so often. Eagles will be at a certain height, waiting for the jet stream of the air. When the jet stream comes, they spread their wings and mount the air. That's the way eagles fly. And if you wait upon the Lord, the Spirit of the Lord will come like a jet stream, and you will spread your wings of faith, and mount up. All the mountains will be under you. All the difficulties and the problems will be under you. There you soar towards the sun.

Another translation of this same verse is, "They shall be renewed as the eagles" (see also Psalm 103:5, "your youth is renewed like the eagle's"). According to a Jewish rabbinical tradition (this is not science; this is just a tradition), every ten years, an eagle will soar towards the sun until it is scorched, and then it will fall into the sea. When it hits the sea, it will molt, will have new feathers, and then rise again. They say this will happen ten times in an eagle's life. After ten times, when an eagle is 100 years old, then the eagle will fall to the sea and disappear. Now that's just a tradition.

But we know that eagles do age. Some people say eagles live a long time. To "renew" like an eagle is to molt. The feathers of an eagle will molt. It will shed off the old feathers and take on new feathers; therefore, it becomes like a new eagle. Its strength is ever renewed like an eagle is transformed.

Brothers and sisters, if we wait upon the Lord, He is the God of all comfort. As we wait upon Him, we will be comforted. We will be "molted." We will be transformed. We will be renewed. There will be no oldness, agedness; we shall always be young and fresh. We will mount up with wings of eagles and be renewed like eagles' wings.

And we "shall run and not tire." Looking Godward, we shall mount up with wings as eagles and fly towards Him. Looking usward, we shall run and not tire. Oh, how often we run the race of life, and we get tired. There is a course before us. God has put us in the course. We have to finish our race, and yet in the running, we find ourselves getting tired. If you wait upon the Lord, you shall run and not tire until you reach the end.

And you shall walk and not faint. To walk speaks of our relationship with the world. So far as our life towards the world is concerned, we are walking through the world. And we shall walk on in righteousness and faint not.

So dear brothers and sisters, our God is the God of all comfort. Oh, how He desires to comfort us! Do not give up. Wait upon Him, and you will be comforted.

6—Behold My Servant

Isaiah 42:1-4, 19-21—Behold my servant whom I uphold, mine elect in whom my soul delighteth! I will put my Spirit upon him; he shall bring forth judgment to the nations. He shall not cry, nor lift up, nor cause his voice to be heard in the street. A bruised reed shall he not break, and smoking flax shall he not quench: he shall bring forth judgment according to truth. He shall not faint nor be in haste, till he have set justice in the earth: and the isles shall wait for his law. ...

Who is blind, but my servant? and deaf, as my messenger whom I sent? Who is blind as he in whom I have trusted, and blind as Jehovah's servant, —seeing many things, and thou observest not? With opened ears, he heareth not. Jehovah had delight in him for his righteousness' sake: he hath magnified the law, and made it honourable.

We mentioned before that this second part of the book of Isaiah, chapters 40-66, has a distinctively clear theme—the salvation of the Lord. The salvation of the Lord means more than the Lord's *way* to save people. The salvation of the Lord is centered upon a Person. In other words, the salvation of the Lord is in the Savior himself, is in Christ himself. Christ himself *is* the way; He *is* the salvation of the Lord. Therefore, in this section of Isaiah, there are many prophecies concerning this Savior and this salvation—our Lord Jesus.

In chapter 42, our Lord Jesus is here called the *Servant* of the Lord. Before, in chapters 7 and 9, He was prophesied as the Son coming to be the Messiah, and now in chapter 42, He is called "My Servant." He *is* the Son of God, and yet He took upon himself the form of a servant. This reminds us especially of Philippians chapter 2. There we read how He who is the Son, being equal with God (and that is not something to be grasped at), emptied himself, taking the form of a bondslave (see vv. 6-8).

When the Lord Jesus came into this world, when He became a man on this earth, He came as a servant of the Lord. He is *the* Servant of the Lord. He came to serve God His Father, and He came to serve God's purpose in all His ways and all His life. So in Isaiah chapter 42, our Lord Jesus is prophesied and described as the Servant of God.

My Servant—Israel

> But thou, Israel, **my servant**, Jacob, whom I have chosen, the seed of Abraham, my friend —thou whom I have taken from the ends of the earth, and called from the extremities thereof, and to whom I said, **Thou art my servant**, I have chosen thee and not rejected thee, —Fear not, for I am with thee; be not dismayed, for I am thy God: I will strengthen thee, yea, I will help thee, yea, I will uphold thee with the right hand of my righteousness (Isaiah 41:8-10).

In studying Isaiah, there is a kind of confusion with this term, *My servant.* It refers to the Lord Jesus the Messiah sometimes, and other times it refers to the nation of Israel that was chosen by God to be His servant. Sometimes it is difficult to separate these two. You have to read the context very carefully in order to know whether *My servant* is referring to Christ or Israel. God raised up the nation of Israel as a corporate servant of His. His purpose in choosing Israel was more than just for the sake of Israel; it was for the sake of the whole world that God might teach the nations through His servant Israel. But Israel was not faithful to God. She not only couldn't teach the nations, but she adopted all the customs and idolatry of the nations. And because of that, God raised up a servant, a true servant in the person of Jesus Christ. Through that Servant, God is able to accomplish what He had meant for Israel to do. Because of His work, eventually, the nation of Israel will again be restored into the position of God's servant. In the millennium, the nation of Israel shall teach all the nations on this earth.

God's Servant—the Church

> And no curse shall be any more; and the throne of God and of the Lamb shall be in it; and his servants shall serve him (Revelation 22:3).
>
> ... ye turned to God from idols to serve a living and true God (I Thessalonians 1:9).

We know that our Lord Jesus is *the* Servant of God. He is the model, the Servant of God. And through Him, salvation is fully accomplished. But we who are redeemed of the Lord individually are all God's servants. We are not only God's children saved by grace, but we are also God's servants. And the church is the corporate servant of God. God has a definite work for the church to do, but the church will never be able to fulfill her mission unless she is fully joined to the Head. Christ is the Head, and the church is His body. Together they are *the Servant* of the Lord. Christ is the Servant of the Lord, and the church in union with Christ also becomes God's servant. Christ is not only our model, our example, but He is the very life and power of our service. So in one sense, this term is applied not only to Christ but also to His church. It is almost inseparable.

The Servant of God—Our Lord Jesus

> Behold my servant whom I uphold, mine elect in whom my soul delighteth! (Isaiah 42:1a)

In seeing Christ as the servant of the Lord, we may learn something of the meaning of servanthood. What does it mean to be God's servant or servants? What is meant by servanthood? We can see this fully expressed and realized in the person of our Lord Jesus.

Behold ...

Whenever you find the word *behold* in the Bible, it is used to arrest our attention. Oftentimes, our attention is rather divided. It is very difficult for us to concentrate because we have too many interests. But here the Spirit of God is calling us to concentrate our attention, to behold—that is, to see, to look at—one Person so that all the other people will just disappear from our view.

Behold my servant

God wants us to forget everybody else, even forgetting ourselves, and God wants us to see His servant in the person of our Lord Jesus—"Behold my servant." What a servant He is! Our Lord Jesus is servant to nobody else. His whole life is occupied with one thing—His Father's business (see Luke 2:49 KJV). He is the faithful and true servant of God (see Revelation 19:11).

Behold my servant, whom I uphold

And because He is sent by God, as God's servant, God backs Him up all the way; He *upholds* Him. Dear brothers and sisters, if we are true servants of God, if we truly serve God with our whole hearts, if we are sent by Him, then the Lord Jesus said:

> Ye have not chosen me, but I have chosen you, and have set you that ye should go and that ye should bear fruit, and [that] your fruit should abide, that whatsoever ye shall ask the Father in my name he may give you (John 15:16).

We are chosen by our Lord Jesus to be His servants—individually and corporately—to bear fruit for Him. And because of that, He will uphold us. No master will send out a servant without backing him up all the way. Suppose you send out someone as your servant who faithfully serves your purpose. Yet when he comes to a time of trouble and difficulty, you back out and say you have nothing to do with him. Now, what kind of a master would you be? Dear brothers and sisters, if we are faithful to the Lord as His servants, we are confident that He will uphold us all the way.

He will never leave us nor forsake us. He will never say, "I have nothing to do with him."

Sometimes He cannot uphold us. Why? Because we have acted on our own. We are not in the spirit of a true servant. A true servant never does anything out of himself. A true servant only does the will of his master. A true servant never seeks anything for himself. But brothers and sisters, sometimes we do. And when we do that, we cannot blame our Master if He does not back us up. But one thing we are sure of, if we are faithful in serving the Lord as His true servants, we know He will uphold us. In fire and in water, He will never leave us. He will never say, "I have nothing to do with them." He says, "Behold my servant, whom I uphold." This principle we find throughout the life of our Lord Jesus. How the Father upholds Him all the way!

mine elect, in whom my soul delighteth!

Our Lord Jesus is elected, chosen by God the Father. Since God has chosen Him, how does He respond to God's election? He responds to God's election with a full commitment of himself. You know, God has also chosen us. We have been elected by God. How do we respond to God's election?

Yesterday, one brother talked to me about this matter of election. Now I have to say, election is a mystery. We may try to explain it to a certain degree, but after all of our explanations, election is God's prerogative. We do not know too much about it. We are told that we are elected in order that our faith may be strengthened. But as to the mystery of election, we are utterly at a loss. That's true.

But dear brothers and sisters, it is not a matter of understanding what the mystery of election is. It is a matter of, having been elected, how do we *respond* to God's election. You are "the elect of God" (Colossians 3:12). But how do you respond to His election? Do you cooperate fully with His election? Do you allow Him to work thoroughly in your life? Do you commit yourself completely to Him to make your election sure? How do you respond to His election?

> ... use diligence to make your calling and election sure, for doing these things ye will never fall (II Peter 1:10).

Look at how our Lord Jesus was elected of the Father and responded with a full commitment. There was no reservation. There was no drawing back. It was a full and complete surrender to the Father's will. And because of that, the Father said, "This is my beloved Son, in whom I have found my delight" (Matthew 3:17). This happened when our Lord Jesus went into the water to be baptized. He had no need to be baptized because there was no reason for Him to repent. There was nothing for Him to repent of. We all need to repent often, all the time. But there was nothing for our Lord Jesus to repent of. Yet He was willing to go into the water to receive the baptism of John, which is the baptism of repentance. Why? He did that in obedience to the Father, offering himself as a substitute for the sins of this world. So when He came out of the water, the heavens opened (see v. 16). And there was a voice from heaven saying, "This is My beloved Son, in whom is My delight." Why? Because there was a full commitment to the Father. A response to that election.

Dear brothers and sisters, God has chosen us to serve Him, but how do we respond to that election? Do we "present [our] bodies a living sacrifice"? Which is "holy, acceptable" to Him? And this is our "reasonable service"? (Romans 12:1) If so, then our Lord can also say, "My good and faithful servant, in whom is My satisfaction."

I will put my Spirit upon him

The Lord Jesus was sent by the Father to be *the* Servant of God. But how did He fulfill His mission? How was He equipped? "I will put my Spirit upon him" (Isaiah 42:1b). Being sent as a servant, the one indispensable piece of equipment is the Holy Spirit. Again, after our Lord Jesus was baptized, as He came out of the water, the Holy Spirit descended as a dove upon Him. And we are told that not only did the Spirit descend as a dove upon Him, but He *abode* in Him (see John 1:32).

Throughout His work on earth as a servant of God, our Lord Jesus did everything in the power of the Holy Spirit. He never did anything on His own. He never did anything by himself. Whenever He did anything, He did it in the power of the Holy Spirit.

In Isaiah 61, the Servant is *anointed* of the Lord.

> The Spirit of the Lord Jehovah is upon me, because Jehovah hath anointed me to announce glad tidings unto the meek; he hath sent me to bind up the broken-hearted, to proclaim liberty to the captives, and opening of the prison to them that are bound; to proclaim the acceptable year of Jehovah (vv. 1-2a).

He said, "the Spirit of God is upon Me, He has *anointed* Me to preach the glad tidings to the poor, to release those that were imprisoned, to open the eyes of the blind, to proclaim the glad tidings, the Jubilee of the Lord." And all of these things were done in the power of the Holy Spirit.

The one indispensable "piece of equipment" that we must have to serve the Lord is the Holy Spirit. Thank God we do have the Holy Spirit. When we believe in the Lord Jesus, the Holy Spirit comes, quickens our spirit, makes it a new spirit, and then He dwells in our new spirit so that the Holy Spirit and our spirit bear witness together that we are children of God (see Romans 8:16). Not only must we have the Holy Spirit, but the question is, are we *filled* with the Holy Spirit? That is to say, are we *ruled* by the Holy Spirit? Do we give ourselves so fully to the Lord that the Holy Spirit has full control over our lives? Are we anointed by the Holy Spirit?

In the Old Testament time, before the priest, the king, and the prophet could function as a priest, king, or prophet, they must be anointed with oil. And even in the Tabernacle, before its utensils could be used, they must be first anointed with oil. The meaning of this is that through the anointing of the oil, everything is quickened into its spiritual reality. Can we serve God if we are not equipped with the Holy Spirit? How can we serve God if we are not *quickened* by the Holy Spirit? How can we serve God if we are not *anointed* by the Holy Spirit? How can we serve God if our lives are not under the *rule* of the Holy Spirit? How can we serve if we are not *led* by the Holy Spirit? It is in the *power* of the Holy Spirit and His *wisdom* that we can serve God's purpose.

If you want to do any other kind of service, you may need to get prepared for it by education, training, or other means.

But in serving God, the one indispensable preparation is not education; it is the Holy Spirit. This doesn't mean that education or training or other things do not help. They may be useful, or they may not be. But the one indispensable thing is the Holy Spirit.

So dear brothers and sisters, as we are chosen of God to be His servants, how we need to be filled with the Holy Spirit, how we need to yield our life to the Lord, that the Holy Spirit may have full control of us. And with that equipment, we will be able to serve God's purpose.

he shall bring forth judgment to the nations.

What was our Lord Jesus sent for? He "shall bring forth judgment to the nations." When we read the word judgment, our reaction will often be, "Well, He is coming to judge the world!" Yes, He is coming to judge the world. But the word *judgment* here in the original Hebrew language means *absolute* and, therefore, *divine right*. So this verse can be translated as "He shall bring out the right among the nations."

What is it that our Lord Jesus was sent into this world for? He was not sent into the world just to judge the world. One day He *will* judge this world. But even when He was in this world, 2,000 years ago, He said, "I do not come to judge the world, I come to save the world" (see John 3:17). One day He will judge the world, but what was it that He was sent for? He is to bring out the right of God toward the nations. God has a divine right. God has authority. He has a divine right over the nations, over the whole world. But this divine right of God is being neglected and opposed. And the coming of Christ was to bring that right out upon the nations. In other words, His work is to bring in the kingdom of God.

As you read on in Isaiah 42, He indeed is

> to open the blind eyes, to bring forth the prisoner from the prison, them that sit in darkness out of the house of restraint (v. 7).

That is true. This is the negative side of His work. On the negative side, His work is "to open the blind eyes," to open the gates of the prison. We were all imprisoned by sin, and He opened the gates and set us free. That is true. But brothers and sisters, this is only the negative part of His work. There is a positive meaning to His work, and the positive meaning is that He is to bring the rule of God over our lives. He is to bring in the kingdom of God. The right of God among the nations. This is His supreme work.

That is the reason why, as you read the Gospels and the book of Acts, you find the kingdom of God is so prominent. What is the gospel of Jesus Christ? The gospel of Jesus Christ is more than just saving people out of hell. The gospel of Jesus Christ is the kingdom of God. Christ comes to bring in God's kingdom among men, to establish His kingdom in the midst of man. What is the kingdom of God? It is the *right* of God, the rule of God, as the law of our life. That is the law of the kingdom.

Thank God we are saved. Thank God He has opened our blind eyes. Thank God He has opened the prison gates and set us free. But does this mean that since we are set free, we are free to do anything we like? After all, you will go to heaven. Does this mean you can practice licentiousness? No. Not at all. Not at all. No, we are set free that we may become "bondmen to righteousness." We are set free that we may come under the rule of God, that the right of God may be upon us, that we may become His kingdom, that our lives may be governed by His rule. And as He begins to manifest His kingdom among His own redeemed people, one day, His kingdom shall appear publicly in this world. How important it is for us today to be put under the rule of Christ! This is God's divine right. He has that right over the whole creation. And He will have that right realized one day.

He shall not cry, nor lift up,
nor cause his voice to be heard in the street.

How does He do this work? Does He try to force His way through? Does He try to accomplish His work by force? By argument? By raising His voice? By being noisy? Not at all. "He shall not cry, nor lift up, nor cause his voice to be heard in the street" (v. 2).

In accomplishing this tremendous work of bringing the kingdom of God to this world, He shall not cry, nor lift up, nor cause His voice to be heard in the street! In other words, He does His work quietly but persistently. This verse is quoted by Matthew when our Lord Jesus healed many people, but He told them not to broadcast these miracles (see 12:16-21). Why? He did not seek His own glory. He only sought the glory of the Father. He only sought to see that the Father's will be done. He did not want to draw people to himself. He did not seek fame or popularity. He did not want to be made known. He did not lift up His voice; He just worked quietly to accomplish the Father's purpose.

Do we need to be argumentative? Do we need to be noisy? Do we need to use force? Not at all. The Spirit of God, when He is working, is quiet and persistent. The work shall be done.

A bruised reed shall he not break

How does He do the work?

> A bruised reed shall he not break, and smoking flax shall he not quench: he shall bring forth judgment according to truth.

Oh, how gentle He is! When we see a bruised reed, our natural temptation will be to break it! What's the use of a bruised reed? Break it, be finished with it. When we see smoking flax, our natural reaction will be to blow it out. What's the use of a *smoking* flax? It gives much annoyance. It does not serve any purpose. So why not just be finished with it? Now that is the human reaction.

A bruised reed represents what appears outwardly. A smoking flax represents what is there inwardly. How true it is that we are all bruised reeds. We are oppressed by sin, bruised, and broken. Inwardly, we are smoking flax. Our life is going out. There is not much life in us. And yet our Lord Jesus will not break a bruised reed. He will not blow out a smoking flax. Instead, He will restore that bruised reed, and He will restore that smoking flax. This is the work of our Lord Jesus. How gentle, how kind, how patient He is!

He shall not faint nor be in haste

Despite all discouragements and disappointments, "He shall not faint." He is sustained by the Father. And He is never "in haste." We often faint, and we are in haste! "There is so much to do. How can we do it? Why is it not done!" We get so excited, and we want to do something. We get so noisy. We get so upset—"impossible!" The more we are like that, the less it can be done. But our Lord Jesus never faints nor is in haste. He just keeps on until the right of God is known throughout the earth. And thank God, it shall be done.

Who is blind, but my servant?
and deaf, as my messenger whom I sent?

There is another side of that Servant, which I would like to mention very briefly.

> Who is blind, but my servant? and deaf, as my messenger whom I sent? Who is blind as he in whom I have trusted, and blind as Jehovah's servant, —seeing many things, and thou observest not? With opened ears, he heareth not. Jehovah had delight in him for his righteousness' sake: he hath magnified the law, and made it honourable (Isaiah 42:19-21).

Most commentators commenting on this section think that the *servant* here refers to Israel, not to Christ. Unfortunately, I do not agree with them. I may be wrong, but as I read this, I feel this section is still referring to Christ. Why? Because of verse 21:

> Jehovah had delight in him for his righteousness' sake: he hath magnified the law, and made it honourable.

Now, Israel hasn't done that. But what goes before this verse is so strange that it seems impossible to be applied to Christ! That's the reason why this passage is always applied to Israel.

"Who is blind, but my servant?" Of course, Israel is blind. "Who is ... deaf, as my messenger whom I sent?" Israel is deaf, that's true. "Who is blind as he in whom I have trusted, and blind as Jehovah's servant, —seeing many things, and thou observest not? With opened ears, he heareth not." We will say, "This is certainly a perfect description of Israel. And it's a perfect description of us too." But dear brothers and sisters, because of verse 21, I cannot accept that. I feel it still refers to Christ.

Is Christ blind? Is Christ deaf? Surely He has His eyes wide open to the Father; He has His ear pierced towards the Father. Every morning the Father will speak to Him—no doubt about that. He has the keenest eyesight; He has the clearest hearing—no doubt about that. But, is it not also true that as God's perfect Servant, He is totally blind and deaf to what the world may say or what He may see in the world?

If you are God's servant, you no doubt will hear a lot from the world. You, no doubt, will see a lot of the world. And what you hear and see will really make you faint. How many of God's servants are discouraged unto despair because of what people say about them and about their work?—because of what they have seen in this world? Oh brothers and sisters, if you see too much and if you hear too much, you are finished!—you cannot go on serving the Lord faithfully. If you want to serve the Lord faithfully, you have to be as blind and deaf as our Lord was. Not blind and deaf to God, but blind and deaf to the world. You have to see as if you haven't seen. You must hear as if you haven't heard. Then you can go on with the Lord.

That is another aspect of the servant of the Lord. As God's servants, how we need to be blind and deaf to what the world may say or may appear to be. We only see the Lord. We only hear the Lord.

Once in a railway station in the East, as the people came out of the station, an inspector stood at the gate and asked for everyone's tickets. As they came out of the train, they had to give him their tickets. It was a very cold day, and people were streaming out of the train. This conductor or inspector was standing there, asking for tickets. Some people had put their tickets in their pockets or even in their bags. And it was so cold. People had to take off their gloves and try to search for their tickets. So everybody was doing that and giving him an evil look. Some said, "Do you think I would take the train without a ticket!?! Don't you trust me?" But no matter what the people said, he just said, "Ticket? Ticket?" As he was doing this, people cursed him. "It is so cold, and you have to demand the ticket?"

One passerby saw the whole thing, so when he came to the conductor, he said, "This must be a real trial to you." "Oh," he said, "No, not at all." And the conductor turned his eyes to look up. In the house above them, the station-master was looking down at him with a smiling face. He said, "That's it. That's it for me." In other words, he just saw the station-master; that's all. When he saw his smile, he didn't care what people said, and he didn't care what he saw. He was blind and deaf.

As God's servants, that is the attitude we have to have towards the world. Not that we are so proud as to not listen to any constructive criticism. We should be humble enough for correction. If there is something wrong, we should confess and change. But so far as God's purpose is concerned, we have to be looking to the Lord and to Him alone.

So dear brothers and sisters, this is the Servant of God—fully manifested in the life of our Lord Jesus. And having His life in us, being in union with Him, God calls us to be His servants and His corporate servant. May the Lord help us.

7—Who Hath Believed Our Report?

Isaiah 52:13-53:12—Behold, my servant shall deal prudently; he shall be exalted and be lifted up, and be very high. As many were astonished at thee—his visage was so marred more than any man, and his form more than the children of men —so shall he astonish many nations; kings shall shut their mouths at him: for what had not been told them shall they see, and what they had not heard shall they consider.

Who hath believed our report? and to whom hath the arm of Jehovah been revealed?

For he shall grow up before him as a tender sapling, and as a root out of dry ground: he hath no form nor lordliness, and when we see him, there is no beauty that we should desire him. He is despised and left alone of men; a man of sorrows, and acquainted with grief, and like one from whom men hide their faces; —despised, and we esteemed him not.

Surely he hath borne our griefs and carried our sorrows; and we, we did regard him stricken, smitten of God, and afflicted. But he was wounded for our transgressions, he was bruised for our iniquities; the chastisement of our peace was upon him, and with his stripes we are healed. All we like sheep have gone astray, we have turned every one to his own way; and Jehovah hath laid upon him the iniquity of us all.

> He was oppressed, and he was afflicted, but he opened not his mouth; he was led as a lamb to the slaughter, and was as a sheep dumb before her shearers, and he opened not his mouth. He was taken from oppression and from judgment; and who shall declare his generation? for he was cut off out of the land of the living; for the transgression of my people was he stricken. And men appointed his grave with the wicked, but he was with the rich in his death, because he had done no violence, neither was there guile in his mouth. Yet it pleased Jehovah to bruise him; he hath subjected him to suffering. When thou shalt make his soul an offering for sin, he shall see a seed, he shall prolong his days, and the pleasure of Jehovah shall prosper in his hand. He shall see of the fruit of the travail of his soul, and shall be satisfied: by his knowledge shall my righteous servant instruct many in righteousness; and he shall bear their iniquities. Therefore will I assign him a portion with the great, and he shall divide the spoil with the strong: because he hath poured out his soul unto death, and was reckoned with the transgressors; and he bore the sin of many, and made intercession for the transgressors.

The portion of Scriptures that we have just read is one of the greatest and most precious portions of the whole Bible. Now, of course, the whole Bible is precious. Every part of it is precious. But there are some portions that seem to speak to us very deeply and very dearly. And that portion which we have just read is among them. I do hope that if you have not yet memorized this portion, you will. We should know this passage by heart. Then we will find how precious it is.

"Who is the prophet referring to?"

These Scriptures refer to someone, and around 800 years after this portion was written, a eunuch of Ethiopia asked about it, "Who is the prophet referring to?" (see Acts 8:34). This Ethiopian eunuch was a proselyte to Judaism, and he had gone to Jerusalem to worship God. After he finished worshipping God in the temple in Jerusalem, he was on his way back to Ethiopia. He was in his chariot reading the Bible, traveling through the desert where there was no man. But as he was reading the Bible, God provided a man to speak to him—Philip the evangelist.

Philip had been laboring in Samaria, and God seemed to bless his evangelism work very much. Many were brought to Christ. It was a very prosperous work of God. But suddenly, an angel of the Lord spoke to Philip to go out of the city and go into the wilderness where there was no one. In obedience to God, Philip went to the desert, and along came this chariot with the eunuch sitting and reading. The Spirit of God moved the heart of Philip to run after that chariot. So Philip just ran along that chariot and turned to that man saying, "What are you reading? Do you know what you are reading?" Sure enough, this man was reading the portion of Isaiah that we have just read:

> He was led as a sheep to slaughter, and as a lamb is dumb in presence of him that shears him, thus he opens not his mouth. In his humiliation his judgment has been taken away, and who shall declare his generation? for his life is

taken from the earth (Acts 8:32b-33 quoting Isaiah 53:7b-8b from the LXX translation).

So when the eunuch was asked by Philip, "Do you understand what you are reading?" he said, "How can I understand? No one is instructing me. I do not know whether the prophet refers to himself or somebody else such as Moses, Abraham, Uzziah, Josiah, Jeremiah, Cyrus, or even Israel." (There are different theories.) "How would I know without anyone explaining it to me. What or whom does he refer to?"

So he asked Philip to come and sit by him in the chariot. As they were going along the way, Philip took up that very Scripture and announced to him the good news of Jesus Christ. And the news was so good! The prophet was referring to the Lord Jesus, who would be born almost 800 years later. He was the one who was wounded for our transgressions. He was the one who was bruised for our iniquities. And with His stripes, we are healed.

Philip announced to the eunuch the glad tidings of Jesus Christ, and the eunuch believed. He asked to be baptized right away. After he was baptized, the Spirit of God took Philip away, and the eunuch went on his way with joy in his heart (see Acts 8:26-40). This was possibly one of the ways God brought the gospel of Jesus Christ into Africa since Ethiopia was in Africa.

This portion of Scripture is very precious. The eunuch had turned to Judaism after he found that all the other religions could not satisfy his heart. He went to Jerusalem to the temple to worship God, to hear the words of the rabbis in Jerusalem. He was reading the word of God, the oracles of God, by himself. But you can see that even after he became a proselyte of Judaism, even after he worshiped God in the temple Jerusalem, even after he had heard the teachings of the great rabbis of those days, there was no understanding. He was still seeking. His heart was still empty. He still was not satisfied until the good news of Jesus Christ was announced to him. Immediately his heart entered into rest, and he was full of joy.

Dear brothers and sisters, it is true that this portion of Scripture does not speak of Isaiah, the prophet. He does not refer to himself. He is not worthy of this description. This cannot be applied to anybody else. It cannot be applied collectively to the nation of Israel, either. This portion is a prophecy concerning our Lord Jesus Christ. He is the only one in the whole universe who fulfills everything that is mentioned in this prophecy.

The Person of the Son-Servant of God

In the preceding chapters, we have already seen that so far as His origin is concerned, our Lord Jesus is the Son of God, and He came to this world to become the Servant of God. The Son became the Servant. And the Son was sent into this world to accomplish a great work. He came to establish the kingdom of God on earth. That was what He came for.

Now in this portion of Isaiah, He is again described as the Servant of God, but there is a difference. The difference here is that the emphasis is on this Person. Who is this Servant of God? What kind of life does He live? How much does He suffer? And why does He suffer? What is the result of His suffering? What does He accomplish through His suffering? And after He has suffered, how does God exalt

Him? In other words, in this passage, we are shown the *Person* of the Son-Servant of God.

Reconciling Suffering with Glory

The theme of Isaiah 52-53 is His sufferings and exaltation. The Jews throughout the centuries couldn't understand this one thing: How could the promised Messiah suffer and be glorified at the same time? They couldn't solve this puzzle. And because of that, when they read the prophecies in the Old Testament, they did not know to whom to apply the sufferings. They knew the Messiah would come, and he would be glorified, and yet the prophecy also prophesied of his suffering. They just couldn't understand it. That's the reason why they sometimes said these verses refer to the nation of Israel. Or this refers to some man of God. They just couldn't understand. Even throughout the centuries the Jews couldn't understand.

> Ought not the Christ to have suffered these things and to enter into his glory? (Luke 24:26)

Even the disciples at the time of our Lord Jesus, who were Jews, couldn't understand. After the Lord was crucified and raised from the dead on the third day, news was brought to the disciples that the Lord had risen. They just couldn't understand it. Two disciples of our Lord Jesus were so discouraged, so disappointed that they left Jerusalem. And as they were walking on the way to Emmaus, they talked about the things that happened in Jerusalem—that Christ was crucified and some women had said that He has risen from the dead. They just couldn't understand it.

Suddenly a man came and walked with them, asking, "What are you talking about?" They said, "Well, you must be a stranger in Jerusalem because this is the subject of conversation everywhere. One whom we considered as the Prophet, as the Hope of Israel, was crucified. And yet some women said He has risen from the dead. And we just cannot understand it." Remember, these are disciples. They couldn't reconcile the whole thing. Our Lord Jesus reprimanded them and said, "Oh, you are so foolish and dull of heart. Ought not the Christ suffer and *then* enter into His glory?" And the Lord began to expound to them the Scriptures. When He expounded the Scriptures to them, their hearts were warmed (see Luke 24:13-32).

Brothers and sisters, the Christ—the One whom God sent to be the Savior of the world—must first suffer and *then* enter into His glory. Our Lord Jesus is the eternal Son of God. In eternity past, He shared the glory with His Father. But then He emptied himself. He left the glory. He humbled himself to become a man. But one day, He returned to His glory. He returned not only to the glory that He shared with His Father in eternity past but also the glory that He earned for himself as the Savior of the world. To earn for himself that glory—the glory of the Redeemer—He had to go through sufferings. His sufferings on the cross accomplished the work of redemption.

So this portion of Isaiah speaks to us of this great theme:

The Messiah's Sufferings and His Exaltation

Behold, my servant shall deal prudently; he shall be exalted and be lifted up, and be very high (Isaiah 52:13).

Behold ...

Each time the Spirit of God uses the word *behold* in the Bible, He is trying to catch our attention. We are so careless. Our eyes are not single. Our ears are hearing different things at the same time. We are so divided. We do not concentrate, and because of this, what we see and hear just passes by. It evaporates and vanishes. Nothing remains.

The Spirit of God is trying to arrest our attention. He is calling us to concentrate and focus on one thing:

Behold, my servant ...

He wants us to see the Lord Jesus as His own Servant. The Father is always trying to draw people's attention to His Son. God is always trying to draw us to see His Servant. In other words, how we need to see the Lord Jesus!—just as the disciples on the Mount of Transfiguration needed to. God dismissed Moses, and God dismissed Elijah so that the eyes of the disciples might see the Lord Jesus and only the Lord Jesus (see Matthew 17:1-9). Let every man be dismissed! Let us see the Lord Jesus this morning and Him alone.

Behold, my servant shall deal prudently

The Lord Jesus, sent by God, will deal prudently, wisely. He will accomplish the will of God wisely and prudently. He is harmless as a dove, but wise, very wise. Wise—not in the sense of being very clever, as we say. In this world, if you are worldly-wise, worldly-clever, or worldly-prudent, how will you conduct yourself? A man who is wise and prudent in the worldly sense is very slippery. You just cannot get hold of him. He will maneuver himself in such a way that he always protects himself. He will not be touched, reached, or harmed.

That is worldly-wise and prudent. In the world, it is foolish to be frank and open because you will be caught and hurt. But this is not the meaning here.

"Behold, my servant shall deal prudently" is not the earthly prudence; it is heavenly wisdom. Our Lord Jesus is so wise, so prudent, that He alone can accomplish the task that God sent him to accomplish. And because He acts so wisely and does everything so well, the result is,

he shall be exalted and be lifted up,
and be very high.

That is the outcome. He was faithful to the Father and prudent in finishing His job, so God highly exalted Him, and He became very high. This is an introduction for us to this servant of God, even our Lord Jesus.

As many were astonished at thee

> As many were astonished at thee—his visage was so marred more than any man, and his form more than the children of men (v. 14).

This servant of God was so prudent and would one day be highly exalted. Yet when He came to this earth, many were surprised or "astonished" at Him. They just couldn't believe. Why? Because He did not come according to man's way. If a great man were coming into this world, we would expect him to be born of nobility. He should be born in Jerusalem, in the palace there. He should be one who was highly educated. He should be a man of great stature. We have our concept of greatness, but as the Lord came into this world, He just did not fit with the worldly concept of greatness. He was born in a manger, not in the palace. He was reared in Nazareth, that hilly country: "Can anything good come out of Nazareth?" (John 1:46) Only the "bad" came out of Nazareth. He had never been to school, that is, to the rabbinical school.

He did not fit with the idea of the Messiah according to the Jewish concept. Why? Because the Jews expected that when the Messiah came, he would overturn the Roman Empire and make the Jewish nation the greatest nation in the world. Yet our Lord Jesus would not touch that. He said, "Render to Caesar the things that belong to Caesar and the things of God to God" (Mark 12:17). He did not fit with the Jewish concept of the Messiah, and for that reason, they rejected Him. In every respect, He was a surprise to many.

The world has a kind of image, a sort of concept of what the Messiah should be, and He just does not fit in anywhere. He is different, unique. He became a surprise to many.

his visage was so marred
more than any man

Artists all have their own concept of Christ. We have seen many paintings of Christ, but actually, these are the artists' concepts. No one alive has seen Christ, and no picture was left of Him. How did Christ look when He was on this earth? Nobody knows. The Scripture does not give us too much description of Him. So all the paintings that you see actually are the artist's idea of the Christ. They painted the face of Christ in all kinds of ways. These are their ideas. They think, "Oh, He is love." And because He is love, some painters paint Him almost feminine. Or they think, "Oh, He is full of righteousness." And they paint Him like a judge. There are all kinds of paintings, but actually, none are the reality. When the Lord Jesus was on earth, what was His visage? What was His appearance? "His visage was so *marred* more than any man." To be literal, this means that His figure, His visage, His physical appearance was so marred that He did not even look like a man.

When Christ was born, He must have been a beautiful baby; no doubt, every baby is beautiful. When Christ grew up, well, He might not be handsome, but He couldn't be ugly because He was to be a man just like we are.

> For he shall grow up before him ... he hath no form nor lordliness, and when we see him, there is no beauty that we should desire him (Isaiah 53:2).

So I do not think He was extraordinarily handsome, but He wouldn't be very ugly either. He must have been common. Just like a common boy. Not too ugly, not too handsome. Just common.

He must have looked common, and yet the Bible says His visage was so marred. He suffered so much. The wear and tear of His life, the hardship, the tribulation, the persecution, the sorrow, the grief, these things came into His life so much that His whole visage was destroyed, was marred beyond human recognition. He did not look like an average human.

On the cross—with the crown of thorns, with His body scourged, with His hands and feet nailed—there on the cross, He didn't look like a man at all. Think about it. Think of the sufferings … the sufferings. We just cannot comprehend the sufferings that our Lord Jesus went through for our own sake. His "visage was marred more than any man." He didn't look like a man anymore.

and his form more than the children of men

It is no wonder that when He was 30, people thought He was 50 (see John 8:56-57). No wonder the two thieves that were crucified with Him lingered on their crosses longer. Their legs had to be broken to speed up their deaths. But our Lord Jesus was only on the cross for six hours, and He died (see John 19:30-33). His body was so bruised. His body was so fragile. His body had suffered so much that in only six hours, He was gone. These are the sufferings of Christ.

—so shall he astonish many nations

There is yet another surprise. He was a surprise or astonishment at first because He didn't fit in with our concept of greatness. He was even almost the opposite of it. And yet after He has accomplished the work of redemption, He again becomes a surprise to the nations. Why? Because the work of salvation has been accomplished, and now many shall come and bow at His feet.

This phrase, "so shall he astonish [or, surprise] many nations," can be rendered another way:

> So shall he sprinkle many nations (KJV)

This word, translated as *sprinkle,* has a special meaning. In the Old Testament time, the priest would sprinkle the blood on the lepers to make them clean. So here in Isaiah 52, since our Lord has suffered so much for us, we have His blood. His blood is sprinkled upon many nations, and many shall be washed clean. They shall be washed clean! That is a surprise.

what had not been told them shall they see,
and what they had not heard shall they consider.

How true this is! The story has never been fully told, even today. What we have heard, what we have seen is something that we can try to understand, but there is much more to it. The story has never been fully told—the salvation of our Lord Jesus. This is Christ.

Who hath believed our report? and to whom
hath the arm of Jehovah been revealed?

The apostle John quoted this:

> But though he had done so many signs before them, they believed not on him, that the word of the prophet Esaias which he said might be fulfilled, Lord, who has believed our report? and to whom has the arm of the Lord been revealed? (John 12:37-38).

He said, "Who believed? And who will receive?" And Paul in Romans, chapter 10 quotes this again:

> But they have not all obeyed the glad tidings. For Esaias says, Lord, who has believed our report? (v. 16)

Who believes our report? This good news of the Lord Jesus—how He suffered and died for us, how He accomplished the work of salvation for us, how anyone who comes to Him shall be sprinkled and be cleansed—who will believe the report? To whom is the arm of the Lord revealed? To whom will the salvation of the Lord come?

Remember, the whole matter is so foreign to our natural mind that unless there is revelation, no one can see it. No one can believe. You need revelation. The Lord Jesus can only be believed in by revelation. As Paul said, "God … was pleased to *reveal* his Son in me" (Galatians 1:16). There must be revelation. If you looked at the outward appearance of the Lord Jesus, there was nothing appealing. No wonder when He was on earth, they despised Him, they rejected Him, there was nothing that appealed outwardly. But if God should open your eyes to see what He is inwardly, then brothers and sisters, it will be a different story.

How we need revelation to know Christ! There is only one way to know Christ—by revelation. And it pleases God to reveal His Son in us. If we only open our hearts to Him, He will reveal His Son to us.

We do not have time now to explain all of Isaiah 53, but I do believe that if you read it yourself, you will see much in this chapter.

as a tender sapling,
and as a root out of dry ground

> For he shall grow up before him as a tender sapling, and as a root out of dry ground: he hath no form nor lordliness, and when we see him, there is no beauty that we should desire him (v. 2).

Oh, how the Lord Jesus, in the eyes of the world, is like a root out of the dry ground! There is no comeliness; there is no lordliness, for us to admire Him. And yet before God, He is a tender sapling.

a man of sorrows,
and acquainted with grief

> He is despised and left alone of men; a man of sorrows, and acquainted with grief, and like one from whom men hide their faces; —despised, and we esteemed him not. Surely he hath borne our griefs and carried our sorrows; and we, we did regard him stricken, smitten of God, and afflicted (vv. 3-4).

He is a man of sorrows and acquainted with grief, but it is *our* sorrow that He bore. It is *our* grief that He carried.

But he was wounded for our transgressions,
he was bruised for our iniquities ...

> But he was wounded for our transgressions, he was bruised for our iniquities; the chastisement of our peace was upon him, and with his stripes we are healed. All we like sheep have gone astray, we have turned every one to his own way; and Jehovah hath laid upon him the iniquity of us all (vv. 5-6).

He was wounded, but for *our* transgressions. He was bruised, but for *our* iniquities. We do not understand! We thought that He was rejected by God. If He pleased God, certainly God would deliver Him from the cross and not allow Him to suffer so much. But we don't realize it was for *our* sake that He suffered all these things, not only from man, but it was God's will that He should so suffer because God has made Him a sin offering for us. But thank God, that is not all.

He shall see of the fruit of the travail of his soul, and shall be satisfied

> He shall see of the fruit of the travail of his soul, and shall be satisfied: by his knowledge shall my righteous servant instruct many in righteousness; and he shall bear their iniquities. Therefore will I assign him a portion with the great, and he shall divide the spoil with the strong: because he hath poured out his soul unto death, and was reckoned with the transgressors; and he bore the sin of many, and made intercession for the transgressors (vv. 11-12).

He shall see of the fruit of the travail of His soul. He shall have a seed, and those who believe in Him shall have their sins forgiven and shall enter into the knowledge of righteousness. God exalted Him and gave Him a name that is above every name—and to that name, every knee shall bow, and every tongue shall confess that Jesus is Lord! (see Philippians 2:9-11)

I do hope that you will continue to read this chapter yourself. Let us remember the sufferings and the exaltation of Christ. Thank God the sufferings are over. He is now exalted at the right hand of the Father, waiting for His enemies to be His footstool (see Hebrews 10:13, Psalm 110:1). This is the Christ we announce, we believe on, and we love.

8—Keep Not Silence, Give Him No Rest

Isaiah 62:1-9—For Zion's sake will I not hold my peace, and for Jerusalem's sake I will not be still, until her righteousness go forth as brightness, and her salvation as a torch that burneth. And the nations shall see thy righteousness, and all kings thy glory; and thou shalt be called by a new name, which the mouth of Jehovah will name. And thou shalt be a crown of beauty in the hand of Jehovah, and a royal diadem in the hand of thy God. Thou shalt no more be termed, Forsaken; neither shall thy land any more be termed, Desolate: but thou shalt be called, My delight is in her, and thy land, Married; for Jehovah delighteth in thee, and thy land shall be married. For as a young man marrieth a virgin, shall thy sons marry thee; and with the joy of the bridegroom over the bride, shall thy God rejoice over thee. I have set watchmen upon thy walls, Jerusalem; all the day and all the night they shall never hold their peace: ye that put Jehovah in remembrance, keep not silence, and give him no rest, till he establish, and till he make Jerusalem a praise in the earth. Jehovah hath sworn by his right hand and by the arm of his strength, I will indeed no more give thy corn to be food for thine enemies; and the sons of the alien shall not drink thy new wine, for which thou hast laboured; for they that have garnered it shall eat it, and praise Jehovah; and they that have gathered it shall drink it in the courts of my holiness.

This is a very wonderful passage! It tells us what God will do for His people and what He expects His people to do. The prophet Isaiah foresaw the captivity of Zion, and he also foresaw the return of that captivity. But as a prophet, he saw even further than that. He saw the days of the Messiah. When the Messiah shall come, everything shall be restored or recovered to the full purpose of God. So what concerned the prophet was not just the immediate need—that is, the return of the Jewish remnant from the captivity of Zion. What really concerned the prophet was the ultimate question—what will happen to Zion and Jerusalem when the Messiah shall come?

The people of Israel were God's earthly people. And today, we who are the redeemed of the Lord are God's heavenly people. God was interested at one time in His earthly people. And God is now interested in us, His heavenly people. So for this time, we are not going through the historical prophecy that concerns the nation of Israel—which *will be* fully fulfilled—but we are concerned with what God determines to do for His people today and what He expects us to do in His work.

For Zion's sake will I not hold my peace,
and for Jerusalem's sake I will not be still ...

Here we read of Zion and Jerusalem. Zion is very dear to God. Jerusalem is very near to God's heart. Zion and Jerusalem in the Scriptures are also spiritually applied to the church today. I don't think we need to be too specific. Still, if you want to be very specific, in typology, Jerusalem represents the church of God, and Zion represents the overcomers of the church. That is found throughout the Bible. Jerusalem represents *all* the people of God, and Zion represents the overcomers of God's people. But I don't think we need to be that specific this time, so we will just put them together as one—Zion and Jerusalem.

God is very jealous over Zion. He is very zealous for Jerusalem. This is His controversy with the nations. It seems as if in God's heart, there is a softness, a tenderness towards Zion and Jerusalem. Now, why of all the cities and mountains, should God have such jealousy over Zion and Jerusalem? The only reason is: God has chosen Zion.

> For Jehovah hath chosen Zion; he hath desired it for his dwelling: This is my rest for ever; here will I dwell, for I have desired it (Psalm 132:13-14).

Out of all the mountains and cities on this earth, God has chosen Zion and Jerusalem to be His dwelling place. It is not because Zion is higher than every other mountain. Nor because Jerusalem is a greater city than any other city. Not at all. It just pleased God. It was the good pleasure of God that He should choose Zion and Jerusalem. And since He has chosen Zion and Jerusalem, He is jealous over that mountain and that city. This is the only reason.

It is not because the children of Israel are better than any other people. As a matter of fact, we find the children of Israel are a very difficult people. They give God lots of headaches and heartaches. And yet God said, "I have chosen Zion. This is My will. My good pleasure. I have chosen it. And since I have chosen it, for Jerusalem's sake and for Zion's sake, I will not be quiet. For Zion's sake, will I not hold my peace. And for Jerusalem's sake, I will not be still." God will not hold His peace until Zion is at peace. God will not be still until Jerusalem is in stillness.

In other words, it does not depend upon the situation and the condition of Zion and Jerusalem. As a matter of fact, Jerusalem, "the city of peace," does not know peace. At the time of this passage, Jerusalem is about to be destroyed and taken into captivity. The people would soon be scattered and the city in ruins. Zion, the place where David dwelt, where the royal scepter ruled, will be scattered. There will be no sign of a royal scepter in Zion. There is no peace in Jerusalem. So far as the people were concerned, it was totally forsaken and desolate.

Is there hope for Zion? Is there any hope for Jerusalem? Is there any hope for these people? Thank God there is. Why? "For Zion's sake I will not hold My peace. For Jerusalem's sake I will not be still. Because I have chosen Zion, I have a purpose for Jerusalem. And until that purpose is fully realized, I will not hold My peace." He said, "I will not be at rest …"

… until her righteousness go forth as brightness,
and her salvation as a torch that burneth.

This is the purpose of God concerning Zion and Jerusalem. Oftentimes, we are confused by our conditions and disappointed by our situation. But if we have the eyes of God, if we can see God's purpose, we will find that God's purpose never changes. Despite the conditions and the situation, God said, "I will …"

> I will [work] until her righteousness shall go forth as brightness, and her salvation as a torch that burneth.

Why? Because this is God's purpose. God's purpose for Zion is that there shall be righteousness; there shall be salvation.

And the nations shall see thy righteousness,
and all kings thy glory ...

As you read on, we see that "the nations shall see thy righteousness, and all kings thy glory." God's purpose for Zion is righteousness, salvation, glory.

... and thou shalt be called by a new name,
which the mouth of Jehovah will name.

Called by a new name!—"which the mouth of Jehovah will name." They shall be marked with a new name.

And thou shalt be a crown of beauty in the hand of Jehovah, and a royal diadem in the hand of thy God.

This is God's purpose. Even a crown of beauty, a royal diadem in God's hand. In other words, God has made Zion a crown of beauty. It is the hand of God that makes Jerusalem a royal diadem. God has made her such that she may be the crown and the diadem upon His head.

Thou shalt no more be termed, Forsaken; neither shall thy land any more be termed, Desolate: but thou shalt be called, My delight is in her, and thy land, Married; for Jehovah delighteth in thee, and thy land shall be married.

In this passage, you have four Hebrew words used as names: *Azubah*, *Shemamah*, *Hephzibah*, and *Beulah*. In some other translations (e.g., KJV, RV, ASV), only the first two names are translated into their meaning, and the other two remain untranslated. I believe they should all be translated or all remain in Hebrew.

Thou shalt no more be termed, Forsaken;

Azubah means *Forsaken.* Azubah is also the name of a woman in the Bible—the mother of Jehoshaphat (see I Kings 22:42).

neither shall thy land any more be termed, Desolate:

Shemamah means *Desolate.*

but thou shalt be called, My delight is in her

Hephzibah means *My delight is in her.* Hephzibah is again a woman's name—the mother of Manasseh (see II Kings 21:1).

and thy land, Married

Beulah means *Married.*

God said, "You shall no longer be called forsaken and desolate, but you shall be called My delight is in you, and you will be married. Not only will your people be married, but I will marry you too!" In other words, the city will be filled with people, and God will take the city as His bride. God himself will be a bridegroom to that city. These are the various descriptions of God's purpose concerning Zion and Jerusalem. And this purpose is glorious.

Now, what is God's purpose with His church today? When we look at the situation today, at the condition of the church, probably we will almost give up. Why? Because, instead of seeing Jerusalem as the city of peace, we find the church full of turmoil. The church is divided. The city is divided. God's people are not together. God's people fight against each other. God's people are in captivity. The testimony of God is weak. There is no royal scepter on Mount Zion.

Brothers and sisters, if we look at this situation, if we look at the condition of God's people today, we will be disappointed because we are not what we should be. We are not what God has purposed us to be. Is there any hope? If it is left to us, there is no hope. If we think of ourselves, it will probably be worse rather than better! There is no hope so far as we ourselves are concerned. But thank God He has not given up. Why? Because God has *chosen* us.

> ... according as he has chosen us in him before the world's foundation, that we should be holy and blameless before him in love; having marked us out beforehand for adoption through Jesus Christ to himself, according to the good pleasure of his will (Ephesians 1:4-5).

Even before the foundation of the world, God has chosen us in Christ Jesus. This is not because we are better than other people in the world, but because it pleases God. It is the good pleasure of God that He should choose us in Christ Jesus. Now, what is the purpose of His choosing us? His purpose in choosing us is that we may "be holy and blameless before Him in love."

What is God's purpose concerning the church? God's purpose concerning the church is that "her righteousness go forth as brightness" (Isaiah 62:1). In Revelation 19, we are told that God's ultimate purpose concerning His church is all realized:

> And it was given to her that she should be clothed in fine linen, bright and pure; for the fine linen is the righteousnesses of the saints (v. 8).

The church is to be clothed with pure linen, white and shining, which is the righteousnesses of the saints. Then again, in chapter 21, we see:

> ... the holy city, new Jerusalem, coming down out of the heaven from God, prepared as a bride adorned for her husband. ... And he carried me away in the Spirit, and set me on a great and high mountain, and shewed me the holy city, Jerusalem, coming down out of the heaven from God, having the glory of God. Her shining was like a most precious stone, as a crystal-like jasper stone (vv. 2, 10-11).

The holy city, the New Jerusalem, descends from heaven, has the glory of God, and her shining is as of precious stones. Brothers and sisters, this is God's purpose concerning His church—that "her righteousness shall go forth as brightness." In other words, the church shall be clothed with righteousness. And since she is clothed with Christ, in union with Christ, and the Holy Spirit is working Christ into her, the result is that she shall be clothed with "the righteousnesses of the saints." The beauty of Christ shall be manifested in brightness in the church. Christ shall be glorified in the church. And "her salvation as a torch that burneth." In other words, the church shall know the salvation of the Lord in such a way that she shall be a testimony—the torch that burneth—to all the world of the salvation of the Lord.

And Revelation 21 further says, "the nations shall walk by its light." By the light of that city! And "the kings shall bring glory to it" (v. 24). So everything that is spoken of concerning Zion and Jerusalem shall be spiritually fulfilled in the church. And indeed, the church shall have a new name, the New Jerusalem. It is not the old Jerusalem because God will make everything new. Everything will be of God. There will be nothing earthly, nothing of man, but everything will be of God and will be new. It will no longer be *Azuba*—Forsaken, but *Hephzibah*—My delight is in her. No longer *Shemamah*—Desolate, but *Beulah*—Married. A Beulah-land "flowing with milk and honey."

Oh, brothers and sisters, sometimes we need to forget our circumstances! We need to close our eyes to our conditions. Not that we try to deceive ourselves. We know only too well our condition and situation. But sometimes, we need to be delivered out from ourselves and see the church from God's viewpoint. See the church according to the eternal purpose of God in Christ Jesus. Oh, brothers and sisters, how we thank God that despite our conditions, despite the situation that we are in today, we know that God is working towards His purpose!

The Lord Jesus said, "I will build My church upon this rock, and the gates of Hades shall *not* prevail against it" (see Matthew 16:18b). The Lord himself said, "*I* will build." He is building. And can He fail? He said, "I will not hold peace! I will give myself no rest! I am working and working until Jerusalem shall be a crown of beauty and a royal diadem." Thank God! Man may fail, but God cannot fail.

> He is faithful who calls you, who will also perform it (I Thessalonians 5:24).

It gives us great encouragement. Think about it.

These words in Isaiah 62 were spoken at least 200 years before the remnant returned and built the city. When those who were in captivity—or even the remnant who returned but were in great distress—heard these words of God, what a comfort, what an uplifting, what a substance for their faith!

Brothers and sisters, this is what it means: we need to see God's purpose concerning His church and how God is determined to realize His purpose in spite of her. Everything will be realized. God takes it upon himself to fulfill His purpose concerning His church. It does not depend on you. It does not depend on me. God takes upon himself the full responsibility of working towards the realization of His eternal purpose. Thank God for that! That takes all our worries and anxieties away.

Yet, when God works, He has a way of working, especially in the new creation. When He created the old creation, He worked alone. He did not ask you to come and join in that work because you were not there yet. None of us were there. He worked all alone. He created the heavens and earth, He created all the things on earth, and He created us. In other words, in the old creation, God worked by himself, and He did it all. But when He works with the new creation, He changed His way. He now refuses to work alone. He *will* work! It is *He* who works, and yet He wants us to join Him in His work. It is a new principle. This is why in the second portion of Isaiah 62, He said:

> I have set watchmen upon thy walls, Jerusalem; all the day and all the night they shall never hold their peace: ye that put Jehovah in remembrance, keep not silence, and give him no rest, till he establish, and till he make Jerusalem a praise in the earth.

I have set watchmen upon thy walls, Jerusalem

In the first portion, God said, "*I* will not hold My peace, *I* will not be still." God said He would work, and He would work until His purpose is fully realized. Then in the second section, we see how He does this work. He said, "I have set watchmen upon thy walls Jerusalem." When God begins to work, He works in man and with man. He sets watchmen on the walls of Jerusalem.

In the old days, every city had a wall surrounding it. They were walled-in for protection. Then they set watchmen on the walls. Why? Because the wall was higher, and the watchmen on the wall would look out over the horizon. Whenever they saw any movement on the horizon, they would immediately cry out and warn the inhabitants within the city. This was their work. The watchmen were placed on the walls on all sides, and they were watching all the time. If there was a slight movement on the horizon, they noticed it and immediately sent out the warning.

God said, "I have set watchmen on thy walls O Jerusalem." When God begins to work, He will set watchmen upon the walls of Jerusalem—He will call some among God's people to serve as watchmen. God has His watchmen. Those watchmen are people who are on higher ground. They are on the walls. They are people who are watching. When other people are sleeping, they are watching. When other people are relaxing, they are in vigilance. Here they are on the walls watching.

Brothers and sisters, when God's people are sleeping or resting, He will apprehend some of His people and set them as the watchmen of the church. God will lift them to higher ground—in the heavenlies! When most of God's people are living on lower ground, as it were, in touch with the world, in such close mixture with the earth, God calls some of them to rise up.

We were dead with Christ, we are raised together with Christ, and we are now seated together with Him in the heavenlies (see Romans 6:8, Ephesians 2:6, Colossians 3:1). God will call His people to come out, come to higher ground, into the heavenlies with Him on the wall.

As you stand with Him on higher ground, then you can see not only the horizon but even beyond the horizon. You can see what is coming; you can see the things that are gathering, and more than that, you can see beyond what is coming—the eternal purpose of God. Oh, brothers and sisters, God needs watchmen! God is well able to do the work, and yet He needs watchmen in the church. Are we willing to pay the cost to be watchmen? Are we willing to be watching while others are resting? Are we willing to climb to higher ground to stay in the heavenlies with Christ that we may be able to see further than other people?—that we may not only see what is coming, but what is way beyond the horizon—the eternal purpose of God. God is calling for watchmen. The watchmen here in Isaiah 62 have more duties than ordinary watchmen. Why? Because first, they are watchmen—they are to watch. But second, they are intercessors—they are to pray.

all the day and all the night
they shall never hold their peace

They shall never hold their peace. They are not only there watching but watching unto prayer. If we do not watch, we cannot pray—we do not know what to pray for! But if we do watch, then we ought to pray. Why? Because what we have seen will drive us to our knees. If we see and do not give ourselves to prayer, then whatever we have seen ends up as if we haven't seen it.

We can see things, and yet some people really see, and other people see as if they haven't seen. When the Lord saw the multitudes, His heart was full of compassion. He said they were like sheep without a shepherd (see Matthew 9:36). But the disciples didn't see that. They saw the multitude, but that was it. They didn't see. They had no burden; they did not pray. The Lord said, "You should pray that God will send out His people to harvest the field" (see vv. 37-38). Oh, how we need to watch! We are living in a very thrilling time. We are living at the end times. Things are gathering; things are moving. It is a very interesting time. If we watch what is coming to this world and see it in relation to the church and to God's purpose, then we should give ourselves to prayer night and day. Do not hold your peace.

Oh, how we need to pray, to intercede. We are not only watchmen, but we are also intercessors. And we are not only intercessors, but it says,

ye that put Jehovah in remembrance,
keep not silence, and give him no rest

We are remembrancers, giving reminders. In the old days, in the royal court, they had people who were called recorders or remembrancers. They would record all the important events that happened in the kingdom. And they would remind the king from time to time of the promises he made (see II Samuel 8:16, I Kings 4:3). The king sometimes made many promises. He said he would reward a certain person, or he would do a certain thing, but he had so many affairs that he would forget. So in the royal court, there were people who were called remembrancers. They would remind the king. They would record everything and then remind the king, "Now, you forgot to reward a certain person as you had promised."

In the royal court of God, we are called to be remembrancers. Think about it. We are not only watchmen, we are intercessors, and we are also remembrancers of God. Does God need to be reminded? Certainly not. We often forget, but God never does. He never forgets His promises. And yet it pleases Him to set us as His remembrancers.

Who is our remembrancer?—the Holy Spirit. The Holy Spirit, who dwells in us, is our Remembrancer. Oh, how He often reminds us of Christ! He reminds us of the truth. He reminds us of God's word. He so reminds us that it strengthens us. As the Holy Spirit reminds us, we remind God. As He brings God's promises to us, we bring those promises to God and say, "Now Lord, You have said it. Don't forget it. Have it done." Keep not silence and give Him no rest.

God said, "I will not rest" (Isaiah 62:1), and God said, "Give Him no rest" (vv.6-7). God is determined not to rest until He has established Jerusalem and made Jerusalem a praise in the earth. And God said, "Don't give Me any rest. You just remind me day and night. Do not keep silent, but remind Me day and night until I establish, until I make Jerusalem a praise in the earth." Oh, brothers and sisters, what a privilege to remind God!

When you read the Bible, you find from time to time that those who knew God reminded God. Abraham reminded God when God had determined to destroy the cities of Sodom and Gomorrah. God shared His burden with Abraham. Then Abraham drew near and said, "Can a just God do unjustly? If there are 50 righteous men in the city, will You destroy the righteous together with the unrighteous? Will You not spare the city?" (see Genesis 18) Abraham reminded God! He reminded Him of His character: "You are a just God, now don't do anything unjust. That will reflect on Your name." He was a good remembrancer giving good reminders.

Moses reminded God too. When God told Moses, "I will wipe out these people, and I will raise your seed up to be a great nation." Moses drew near and said, "Now God, don't You remember Your name? Your name is 'I am merciful and gracious, ready to forgive.'" And God said, "I have forgiven. I have forgiven" (see Numbers 14:1-20).

Brothers and sisters, we need to remind God. How many of God's people today are really watchmen? How many of God's people today are really intercessors? How many of God's people today are really remembrancers of God? Are we just sitting back and going to sleep? Are we just passively waiting for God to work? That is not God's way of working. True, it is *God* who works, you cannot work, I cannot work, none of us can do anything; no matter what we do or how we do it, it is totally of no use. God said, "I will do it." But God also said, "I need watchmen. I need intercessors. I need remembrancers." Is it because there are no watchmen, no intercessors, and no remembrancers that God's hands are bound? Is this why He cannot work? He does not work because He cannot deny himself. If working together with us is His will, then He cannot deny himself.

Oh, how important it is to see this! On the one hand, we need to see God's purpose. It never changes. Nothing can change God's purpose. His purpose shall be fulfilled—thank God! On the other hand, in connection with that purpose, God needs watchmen. May we give ourselves to the Lord, setting ourselves apart for Him. May we be willing to stay in the heavenlies, on higher ground, watching and praying. Intercede. Remind God of His word, of His promise, of His purpose. As watchmen were raised up, God said:

I will indeed

Once there are watchmen, intercessors, and remembrancers, God says, "All right, I have sworn. I'll do it. I'll do it."

So dear brothers and sisters, may we see God's purpose, and may we join ourselves to that purpose in answering the call of God to be watchmen, intercessors, and remembrancers of God.

9—To the Afflicted and Contrite in Spirit

Isaiah 66:1-2, 5, 7-9, 22-24—Thus saith Jehovah: The heavens are my throne, and the earth is my footstool: what is the house that ye will build unto me? and what is the place of my rest? Even all these things hath my hand made, and all these things have been, saith Jehovah. But to this man will I look: to the afflicted and contrite in spirit, and who trembleth at my word. ...

Hear the word of Jehovah, ye that tremble at his word: Your brethren that hated you, that cast you out for my name's sake, said, Let Jehovah be glorified, and let us see your joy! but they shall be ashamed. ...

Before she travailed, she brought forth; before her pain came, she was delivered of a man-child. Who hath heard such a thing? who hath seen such things? Can a land be made to bring forth in one day? shall a nation be born at once? For as soon as Zion travailed, she brought forth her sons. Shall I bring to the birth, and not cause to bring forth? saith Jehovah; I who cause to bring forth, shall I shut the womb? saith thy God. ...

For as the new heavens and the new earth which I will make shall remain before me, saith Jehovah, so shall your seed and your name remain. And it shall come to pass from new moon to new moon, and from sabbath to sabbath, all flesh shall come to worship before me, saith Jehovah. And they shall go forth, and look upon the carcases of the men that have transgressed against me:

> for their worm shall not die, neither shall their fire be quenched; and they shall be an abhorrence unto all flesh.

We have been taking out some of the passages in the book of Isaiah and meditating on them. We have found that Isaiah was one who knew the salvation of the Lord in such a marvelous way. When we read the book of Isaiah, it is almost like reading the New Testament. Isaiah was a prophet. A prophet is one who knows the mind of God. In his prophecies, he reveals to us what is in the mind of God. Isaiah shows us not only Christ our Redeemer, but he also imparts to us the spirit of redemption. As we come to the last chapter, it is the summing up, the consummation of all the prophecies of Isaiah.

In the first chapter of Isaiah, God called upon the old heaven and the old earth to hear and to bear witness:

> Hear, ye heavens, and give ear, thou earth! for Jehovah hath spoken: I have nourished and brought up children; and they have rebelled against me (v. 2).

Despite all of God's love, the children of Israel rebelled against Him:

> The ox knoweth his owner, and the ass his master's crib; Israel doth not know, my people hath no intelligence (v. 3).

God loved His people very much, and yet they rebelled against Him. So God called upon heaven and earth to bear witness to this. But when you come to the last chapter of

Isaiah, God has made all things new—the new heavens and the new earth. The beloved of the Lord shall dwell in them.

> For as the new heavens and the new earth which I will make shall remain before me, saith Jehovah, so shall your seed and your name remain (Isaiah 66:22).

Man may fail, but God—never. And whatever He has purposed for His people, despite their failures, He will accomplish it to His glory. That certainly should give us great comfort.

In this last chapter, we would like to point out just a few things.

One: What is the eternal purpose of God concerning His people? What does God desire in His people?

No doubt, you will find in the Bible how God desires to dwell among His own people. God wants to find His rest in His own. This theme runs throughout the whole Bible. In the very beginning, after God created Adam, God put man in the Garden of Eden. God came and had fellowship with man.

When the children of Israel were in Egypt as slaves, God raised up Moses to deliver them out of Egypt. They were redeemed in order that they might have a tabernacle where God could dwell among His people. After the children of Israel entered into the Promised Land, God chose David and Solomon to build Him a temple in which His name was placed.

God's purpose with His people has been and is still to dwell among His people. Yet, does God really want a temple? Does God really look for a house built with stones? It is true that God called Moses to build Him a tabernacle. It is true that God chose David and Solomon to build Him a temple. And how the children of Israel looked upon that temple! They considered it as everything to them, and they should. But their view of the temple was such that it was almost an obsession with them. It became a deception to them. It even became a superstition to them. They put so much emphasis on the temple. They thought that as long as they had the temple, as long as they had the sacrifices going on, as long as they had the priesthood, everything was fine. They thought everything was all right. They put their trust in the temple and in their services to it. They thought, "What would God desire more than a house? What could God ask for more than these sacrifices?" As long as they had the temple and they had these sacrifices, God should be happy with them, God should bless them, and God should be with them. It became an obsession, a deception, a superstition!

But does God really want an earthly temple, a physical house?

> But who is able to build him a house, seeing the heavens and the heaven of heavens cannot contain him? (II Chronicles 2:6)

God is greater than the universe that He created. And if the heavens and the heaven of heavens cannot contain Him, how will a little house!?!—though it is built with precious stones and gold—how will *that* accommodate Him?

The heavens are my throne,
and the earth is my footstool

The heavens are where He reigns. The earth is where He carries out His will, His authority. In a sense, heaven and earth are His office, His court. This is where He exercises His authority. This is where He carries out His will. It is His office. The whole universe is His office.

what is the house that ye will build unto me?
and what is the place of my rest?

But, neither the heaven nor the earth is His home, His rest. What is He *really* after? God is not looking for a *physical* house. In the Old Testament time, the tabernacle or temple were just shadows or types. Even with the children of Israel, God was not looking merely for a physical temple. God was looking for a people whose spirit agreed with the meaning of that temple. Once His people lacked that agreement, that temple was nothing.

God spoke through the prophet Isaiah, "The heavens are My throne, and the earth is My footstool, what is the house that ye will build unto Me? And what is the place of My rest? Do you think that just by building a great temple, that is enough for Me? Do you think that this is the place of My rest? Not so." Here is what God is really looking for:

to this man will I look:
to the afflicted and contrite in spirit,
and who trembleth at my word.

Dear brothers and sisters, what is God's house? Where is God's rest? His rest is not in anything physical but something spiritual, not with temples made of stones but with *living* stones—a man with an afflicted and contrite spirit. God will build His home with that kind of spirit. Wherever God can find an afflicted and contrite spirit, He will use that as material to build His house. It is only with that spirit that God can find His rest. This is the eternal purpose of God.

We are the redeemed of the Lord. Thank God for His redemption. But what is the condition of our spirit? What is the attitude of our spirit? Do we exhibit a contrite and afflicted spirit before the Lord? Or do we have a proud and arrogant spirit? Are we self-righteous? Or do we humble ourselves before the Lord? What kind of spirit do we have? God cannot build His house with a proud and arrogant spirit.

> But he giveth more grace. Wherefore he saith, God resisteth the proud, but giveth grace unto the humble (James 4:6 KJV).

What is the "afflicted and contrite" spirit? A spirit that is afflicted—now what is meant by that? It simply means a spirit that can be touched by God and by His word, a spirit that is meek and lowly, a spirit that is humble.

> Blessed are the poor in spirit, for theirs is the kingdom of the heavens (Matthew 5:3).

Here is the foundation stone of the building of God's house—the *poor* in spirit. Poor here is not in the sense of being spiritually nothing, but rather that, in spite of all that God may have given to us, our spirit is yet still poor—not content or self-satisfied. We do not consider ourselves as have arrived, but instead, because of the greatness of His grace, we humble ourselves even lower. We confess that we know nothing, we have nothing, we are nothing. Blessed are the poor in spirit, for theirs is the kingdom of the heavens.

How often we find among Christians a proud, self-righteous arrogancy. With the little grace that they know, they think they know everything. With the little mercy that they have received, they think they have arrived. But brothers and sisters, it is to the man with an afflicted and contrite spirit that God will look.

Why "afflicted"? It simply means that when the word of God comes to that person, it reaches him. It doesn't just go in one ear and out the other. The word of God reaches him. He trembles at God's word. He is wounded, afflicted, bruised, smitten by God's word. His conscience is sensitive. His heart is open. To that kind of spirit will God look for rest.

Since he is afflicted, he is also contrite—he repents before God. Do you think that we do not need to repent? Sometimes we think that only the unbelievers need to repent. They need to repent and believe in the Lord Jesus (see Mark 1:15; Acts 2:38; 3:19). That's true! But in the Bible, the word often comes to us that *we* need to repent (see II Corinthians 7:9-10; II Timothy 2:25; Revelation 2:5, 16; 3:3, 19). How we need to repent again and again before God. When His word smites us, we need to repent before Him with a contrite spirit.

David wrote in Psalm 51, "the sacrifices of God are a broken spirit" (v. 17). God does not look for the sacrifice of a lamb or bullock. God is looking for the sacrifice of a broken spirit—a person who does not stand arrogant before God, but who bows down, broken down before God. This is the material for the building of God's house.

Remember the story of Job. He was a perfect man. He was righteous above all others during his generation. And yet somehow in his spirit, there was a self-righteous spirit—the spirit of a Pharisee. And because of that, God allowed Satan to attack him. Because of that, his spirit was afflicted to the extent that one day he cried out:

> I had heard of thee by the hearing of the ear, but now mine eye seeth thee: Wherefore I abhor myself, and repent in dust and ashes (Job 42:5-6).

That is an afflicted and contrite spirit. And when that spirit is present, the presence of the Lord is manifested. This is where God will rest. As long as we are proud of ourselves, as long as we are arrogant, God cannot rest. But when God finds a spirit that is afflicted, broken, and contrite, even God enters into rest.

This is where God, not to mention we also, come into rest. When we are arrogant, self-righteous, and proud, do we have rest? We don't. We become restless. But when we are afflicted by the Lord, humbled before the Lord, and we yield ourselves completely at His feet, then we come into rest.

What a wonderful thing! A marvelous experience! We come into rest, and in that rest, God too comes into rest. This is what God is looking for. This is His house. This is His rest. This is the material that He will use to build His home in which He will dwell.

Two: What will happen to those with an afflicted and contrite spirit who tremble at the word of God?

First, do we tremble at the word of God? When we hear the word of God, are we able to maintain our integrity? When we hear the word of God, are we able to stand erect with our heads up? Or when we hear the word of God, do we tremble because His word smites us? Does His word find us out?

Hear the word of Jehovah,
ye that tremble at his word

What will happen to those who tremble at God's word? What will happen to those who have an afflicted and contrite spirit? We just saw how God will use such people as material for the building of His house. But what will happen to them? We may think that surely they will be greatly blessed by God. Surely, they will manifest great joy. Surely, the whole world will admire them. Surely, others who belong to the Lord will look up to them and try to imitate them. But not so. What will happen to those who tremble at God's word?

> Your brethren that hated you, that cast you out for my name's sake, said, Let Jehovah be glorified, and let us see your joy! but they shall be ashamed (Isaiah 66:5).

In other words, those who have the spirit of the Lamb will not only be persecuted by the world but even by their own brethren. How strange it is—instead of being admired, instead of being looked up to, your brethren will hate you! They will cast you out. They will ridicule you and say, "Let Jehovah be glorified. You say you want to glorify the Lord; where is the glory? In what respect have you glorified Him? You said you want to please the Lord; where is your joy?"

You will be misunderstood. You will be ridiculed, mocked at. You will be persecuted, even cast out. And that will be your treatment. A slave cannot be higher than his master. Our Lord, our Master, was persecuted and cast out by the world. He was hated even by His brethren in the flesh.

Do you think we who "follow the Lamb whithersoever He goes" will fare better? Not so. We will receive the same treatment.

Oh, brothers and sisters, do not think that because you love the Lord, because you tremble at His word, because you allow His word to do its perfect work in your life, because you have a contrite spirit, that therefore you will be honored and respected. Not so. Instead, you will be tread upon, you will be despised, you will be misunderstood, you will be cast out for the name of the Lord.

> Blessed are ye when they may reproach and persecute you, and say every wicked thing against you, lying, for my sake (Matthew 5:11).

Three: With such treatment, is it all in vain? Not so.

> Before she travailed, she brought forth; before her pain came, she was delivered of a man-child. Who hath heard such a thing? who hath seen such things? Can a land be made to bring forth in one day? shall a nation be born at once? For as soon as Zion travailed, she brought forth her sons. Shall I bring to the birth, and not cause to bring forth? saith Jehovah; I who cause to bring forth, shall I shut the womb? saith thy God (Isaiah 66:7-9).

This is the travail of Zion. Zion in the Scripture always stands for the overcomers, just as Jerusalem stands for the whole church. Here is the travail of Zion. Zion has to travail in order to bring forth "a man-child." Physically speaking, if there is no travail, there can be no birth. Spiritually speaking, this is also true. It is through the travail of the soul of our

Lord Jesus that the church was born. And it is through the travail of the overcomers that the church is brought into maturity.

All the sufferings that you suffer for the sake of Christ are not in vain. They are not just sufferings; they are travailings. As Zion travails, it will bring forth a man-child. This reminds us of Revelation 12, where the woman was in travail, and out of that travail, a man-child was born. That man-child was destined to rule the world with an iron rod. Once the man-child is born and raptured to the throne, there will be war in heaven. Satan will have no place in heaven and will be cast down upon the earth (see vv. 1-9).

Brothers and sisters, the travail of Zion is essential. We may think that Zion travails long and hard, but this is not so, not so. We read:

Before she travailed, she brought forth

It was *before* she travailed that she brought forth her sons. In our feeling, especially while we are in travail, we think that the time is so long. An hour becomes a day; a day becomes a month; a month becomes a year, or maybe a century. But the Bible says,

> For yet a very little while he that comes will come, and will not delay (Hebrews 10:37).

He that is to come will come soon and will not delay. It is for yet a little while, only for a short time, and He that is to come shall come. The travail of Zion is short; it is not long. It is so short that it is as if "before she travail(s)" the child has come.

> Shall I bring to the birth, and not cause to bring forth? saith Jehovah; I who cause to bring forth, shall I shut the womb ? saith thy God (v. 9).

Do you think God will give conception and not let it be brought forth? Certainly not.

> Rejoice with Jerusalem, and be glad for her, all ye that love her; rejoice for joy with her, all ye that mourn over her (v. 10).

Oh, that Zion, the daughters of Zion, may be willing to travail for the purpose of God! Oh that the daughters of Zion may be comforted knowing that their travailing is but for a short while. It is so short that before she travails, she brings forth fruit. Thank God for that.

ye shall be comforted in Jerusalem

It is through the travail of Zion that Jerusalem is brought back into the blessing of God:

> For thus saith Jehovah: Behold, I will extend peace to her like a river, and the glory of the nations like an overflowing torrent; and ye shall suck, ye shall be carried upon the side, and be dandled upon the knees. As one whom his mother comforteth, so will I comfort you; and ye shall be comforted in Jerusalem (Isaiah 66:12-13).

The overcomers in the church are travailing for the sake of the whole church. The church will be brought into maturity through their travail. Then the Bridegroom will come to claim His bride. Oh, brothers and sisters, this is tremendous!

the new heavens and the new earth

Finally, we see how God is working steadily towards His own purpose. As God apprehends for himself a company of overcomers—those who have an afflicted and contrite spirit, those who tremble at His word, those who are called by God to enter into travailing—through their travail, God will bring the whole church into maturity. When the church is fully grown, the Bridegroom will come back to claim her as His bride. Then judgment will follow very speedily upon the nations. And there will be the millennium! And the millennium will soon be passed, and there will be the new heaven and new earth—even eternity.

Brothers and sisters, He who has purposed in the beginning, shall surely perfect and complete it. This is the conclusion of the book of Isaiah.

TITLES AVAILABLE
from Christian Fellowship Publishers
By Watchman Nee

Aids to "Revelation"
Amazing Grace
Back to the Cross
A Balanced Christian Life
The Better Covenant
The Body of Christ: A Reality
The Character of God's Workman
Christ the Sum of All Spiritual Things
The Church and the Work – 3 Vols
The Church in the Eternal Purpose of God
"Come, Lord Jesus"
The Communion of the Holy Spirit
The Finest of the Wheat – Vol. 1
The Finest of the Wheat – Vol. 2
From Faith to Faith
From Glory to Glory
Full of Grace and Truth – Vol. 1
Full of Grace and Truth – Vol. 2
Gleanings in the Fields of Boaz
The Glory of His Life
God's Plan and the Overcomers
God's Work
Gospel Dialogue
Grace Abounding
Grace for Grace
Heart-to-Heart Talks
Interpreting Matthew
Journeying towards the Spiritual
The King and the Kingdom of Heaven
The Latent Power of the Soul
Let Us Pray
The Life That Wins
The Lord My Portion
The Messenger of the Cross
The Ministry of God's Word
My Spiritual Journey
The Mystery of Creation
Powerful According to God
Practical Issues of This Life
The Prayer Ministry of the Church
The Release of the Spirit
Revive Thy Work
The Salvation of the Soul
The Secret of Christian Living
Serve in Spirit
The Spirit of Judgment
The Spirit of the Gospel
The Spirit of Wisdom and Revelation
Spiritual Authority
Spiritual Discernment
Spiritual Exercise
Spiritual Knowledge
The Spiritual Man
Spiritual Reality or Obsession
Take Heed
The Testimony of God
The Universal Priesthood of Believers
Whom Shall I Send?
The Word of the Cross
Worship God
Ye Search the Scriptures

The Basic Lesson Series
Vol. 1 - A Living Sacrifice
Vol. 2 - The Good Confession
Vol. 3 - Assembling Together
Vol. 4 - Not I, But Christ
Vol. 5 - Do All to the Glory of God
Vol. 6 - Love One Another

ORDER FROM: 11515 Allecingie Parkway Richmond, VA 23235
www.c-f-p.com – 804-794-5333

ORDER FROM: 11515 Allecingie Parkway Richmond, VA 23235
www.c-f-p.com – 804-794-5333

TITLES AVAILABLE
from Christian Fellowship Publishers
By Stephen Kaung

Abiding in God
Acts
"But We See Jesus"—*the Life of the Lord Jesus*
Discipled to Christ—*As Seen in the Life of Simon Peter*
God's Purpose for the Family
Government and Ministry in the Local Church
The Gymnasium of Christ
In the Footsteps of Christ
The Key to "Revelation" – Vol. 1
The Key to "Revelation" – Vol. 2
The Master's Training
Ministering the Word of God
Moses, the Servant of God
Nehemiah
New Covenant Living & Ministry
Now We See the Church—*the Life of the Church, the Body of Christ*
Proverbs
Shepherding
The Songs of Degrees—*Meditations on Fifteen Psalms*
The Splendor of His Ways—*Seeing the Lord's End in Job*
Titus

The "God Has Spoken" Series
Seeing Christ in the Old Testament, Part One
Seeing Christ in the Old Testament, Part Two
Seeing Christ in the New Testament